DETERMINED

*A Lifetime of Love and Hate, War and Peace ...
And What the Water Moccasin Taught Me*

FELKER WARD JR.

MR. MEDIA BOOKS
ST. PETERSBURG, FLORIDA, USA

Visit us on the web!
https://MrMediaBooks.com
https://facebook.com/felkerwardjr/

Front and back cover design by Lori Parsells
http://www.VibranceAndVision.com

Mr. Media® is a registered trademark of Bob Andelman
https://MrMedia.com

Manufactured in the United States of America
10 9 8 7 6 5 4 3 2 1

ISBN: 9781731416520

Also available as an e-book.

For
My Parents,
My Wife, Mary,
Our Children
And Grandchildren

Contents

III. CIVILIAN LIFE

IV. FATHER, GRANDFATHER, HUNTER, FISHERMAN

ACKNOWLEDGMENTS

Thank you to my mother and dad, who devoted their lives to the well-being of their children, and who always conveyed the greatest expectation of my undertakings, even as I became the first college graduate in our family; a dad who, after I brought home an all "A" report card, except a "B" in conduct, lamented that, "anybody can make an 'A'" in conduct, all you have to do is keep quiet until you are called upon in class."

To my wife, Mary, who has offered her thorough critique of my story. Mary guides me, our children and our grandchildren, and is the most forgiving person I have ever known. Mary was an ideal Army wife, who readily adjusted to the eight relocations during our 17 years of married Army life. She always, where possible, had a job to enhance our income. During my assignment at Fort Meade, Maryland, Mary worked as a clerk in the Headquarters of the U.S. Army Corps of Engineers. Subsequently, when I was assigned to 8th Army Headquarters in Korea, Mary worked as an administrative assistant to the military law judge in South Korea. On my assignment in Atlanta at Fort McPherson, Mary taught school in the Fulton County school system. At all times, she did an outstanding job of managing our budget to match our income. On those occasions when I decided to pursue a major economic undertaking, her only question was, "When do we get started?" Once, she permitted me to mortgage our home to help finance a business venture I wanted to undertake. (This venture later paid significant dividends, but nonetheless, the business risk was there at the start.) We have been married 58 years. If forgiving gets you to heaven, she'll get a fast pass.

To my children—Michael Ward, Felecia Wynnette Little (Wende), Felker William Ward III (Jay) and Franklin Wesley Ward (Wesley)—who have brought their mother and me the greatest joy a parent could desire. They have brought happiness to our family and our home, and have grown to be fine, outstanding adults, of whom we are very proud. (They also provided their comments and critique as I moved forward with writing this book.)

And to our grandchildren—Maurissa Aarenease Ward, Evan Michael Ward, Morgan Ward, Michaela Ward and Kerrington Austyn Little—we adore each of you and treasure every moment we have spent watching you grow and mature into wonderful young people.

My thanks to my dear friend of many decades, Andy Young, who favored me with an introduction to this memoir. An entire book could be filled with wonderful stories about the good works and friendship of Andy, whom I consider to be a national treasure. We all know him as an icon of the Civil Rights Movement, but he is so much more than that. Andy makes himself available at times of need. He is never too busy to provide his support and assistance wherever it is needed. Andy is a real icon in Georgia—and a personal inspiration to me. He is always working on something for the improvement of his local community and the nation at large.

My gratitude must be shared with my assistant, Mattie Williams, who frequently reminds me that she has been helping me in all of my undertakings for 39 years. She is my right hand and I would be lost without her.

I appreciate the attention to detail provided by Vicki Krueger and Mimi Andelman, the two editors who reviewed my manuscript, as well as the many, many hours of interview transcription work done by Karen Napier. Mary Harper indexed the book and also caught a few last-second typos.

Finally, thank you to Bob Andelman, my co-author in telling this life story. He came highly recommended to me by Sylvia Russell, based on the fine job he did in helping my college roommate—Sylvia's late husband—Herman J. Russell capture his career in "Building Atlanta."

FOREWORD

I met Felker Ward Jr. for the first time when I returned to Atlanta from New York (and Washington, D.C.) at the completion of my tenure as United States Ambassador to the United Nations under President Jimmy Carter.

Felker was a member of a small informal group of citizens, the Action Forum, concerned about the future of our city. The group met for breakfast once a month, and I occasionally met with them to seek their input on important current issues—social, political and economic.

We were mutual acquaintances of Herman Russell and Jesse Hill; the three of them were in business together at Concessions International, and Felker and Herman were college roommates at Tuskegee Institute (now Tuskegee University).

I also knew of Felker because he conducted an aircraft accident investigation in Germany. My sister-in-law's first husband was one of the Army pilots who was killed in the crash. At that moment, he knew more about parts of my family than I did.

Ironically, for someone whose book I am introducing, and for as long as I've known Felker, he has always been someone who kept his business to himself. It wasn't that he was secretive; he just wasn't boastful. And that's probably best in a city like Atlanta, because people tend to envy your success. You could build up enemies if you became too good too quick.

The other thing that I noticed about Felker early on was that he was always comfortable in interracial situations. He was a part of a world I knew nothing about for many years. He understood the cultural complications of business and culture in America long before many of us did. He stayed away from politicized issues, and yet he was close to every politician in town—Democrat or Republican.

Felker's wife, Mary, and my wife, Carolyn, are close, and have known each other for a long time through their Clark College sorority days on through their current social clubs.

We have been close friends for decades, but we've never mixed professionally, whether it was politics or business. One of the reasons that we always got along was that, in order to help grow the Atlanta economy as an integrated, global phenomenon, I could not be a part of it. I could not cross that ethical line, could not be a participant. Nor could anybody in my family. But I was supportive of people such as Jesse and Herman and Felker. I was a friend. But I was never in their business, and they were among the best business people in town.

Once upon a time there were more black PhDs in Atlanta than any other city in the world. That was the basis of the black business coalition that started working together in the 1950s and '60s and brought the long-dominant white business coalition reluctantly to the table in the 1970s. It's been strained, but it's never been broken, thanks to people such as Herman Russell, Jesse Hill and Felker Ward Jr. To this day, that coalition has been the key to Atlanta's interracial successes, financially, politically and socially.

Felker, Jesse and Herman led the generation that took over the coalition in the '70s. They certainly were a significant factor in helping elect me to Congress in 1972. Together, we passed a referendum on a mass transit system, and together we laid the groundwork for a new airport. There was always a black and white partnership.

•••

Felker came to maturity in that period when there was a conscious integration of American military services. He served with honor as an officer and helicopter pilot during Vietnam and, as a retired lieutenant colonel, he spent several decades as Georgia's Civilian Aide to the Secretary of the Army (CASA)—a liaison between the military hierarchy and the citizens of Atlanta and the United States at large.

I understand Felker's military career kept him pretty busy overseas while Dr. Martin Luther King Jr., Ralph Abernathy, Vernon Jordan, Felker's college roommate Herman J. Russell, I and countless others were leading the Civil Rights Movement in the Deep South.

Felker didn't do any marching—you'll find no civil disobedience in his history. And while I didn't know him then, everything I've learned of his 20-year Army career leads me to believe he was breaking down barriers everywhere he traveled in the service of the United States of America.

For example, when he and Herman were seniors at Tuskegee Institute in Alabama, a professor of military science and tactics was also the ROTC's head military official. When the professor decided to reassign a captain that was his subordinate and a favorite teacher of the students, Felker felt this was unfair and led a delegation of students to the college president's office to protest.

And when, in Berlin, his commanding officer intended to relegate Felker—and his career—to the motor pool for no other reason than he was black, Felker defiantly risked his career by putting his foot down and saying, "No!"

If he had been in Atlanta in the 1960s, I have no doubt he would have been standing alongside his friend Herman and the rest of us because it's just been his nature to get involved and stand up against injustice and inequality. He made a difference in his own way from deep within the Establishment.

In many ways, the American military was far ahead of the rest of society. In ranking, it was sports, the military, then business, politics and the church, which was probably last.

In the Civil Rights Movement, alongside Dr. King as I was, we respected and celebrated the men and women who fought our fight on other levels. We happened to be the foot soldiers who were in the streets, and quite often were beaten up and thrown in jail. It paid almost nothing; the top salary in the field was $6,000 a year with no benefits, no insurance, no retirement. But that was our role.

All of our lives we've always known we were fighting battles on multiple fronts. I understood the battle that Felker and his African-American counterparts had in the military.

In the Carter Administration, Cliff Alexander was the secretary of the Army, and he was once sent three lists of possible candidates for promotions to the rank of general. The first list had only one or two black men on it. But the Carter Administration felt that the proportion of black command officers should be similar to the proportion of the troops itself.

The struggle has always gone on, on many levels. And Felker has been involved in several of those levels.

•••

The other thing I want you to know about my friend Felker, Dear Reader, is that while he still is a voracious reader who keeps up with the world around him intellectually, he's never lost his interest in the land and hunting and fishing. Me? Not so much. I'm basically a city boy. I've never done much fishing or hunting at all. But so many people in our city make decisions on the golf course and develop relationships through their sports activities that Felker has always cultivated a network of fellow outdoorsmen, who just happen to be top generals, CEOs or politicians.

He's had close relationships with the broadest diversity of people of almost anybody I know. He knows the poorest of the poor and stays in touch and stays active in his community and church activities, as does his wife. And yet, he doesn't talk about any of it. So unless you're doing an investigative reporting job, it would almost never come up. I have often asked myself, "How can you have somebody that you consider one of your best friends and you know almost everything about them, and yet you know nothing?"

Since I first met Felker in the 1970s, he has always been willing to tackle change and confront racism. It's just that he has always taken action in carefully considered ways that he thought would be most effective. Several generations of Atlanta mayors and Georgia governors have called on him to defuse racial tensions over the years.

Felker's intention is to bring the best out of everyone he meets.

His legendary modesty and humility are among the elements that made him successful. He never looked for credit, never sought the spotlight. He always prided himself on being a behind-the-scenes person.

I always say there's no rest for the wicked, and the righteous don't need it. Felker Ward Jr. never needed rest; when he finished a task before him, he was always in search of the next mountain to climb.

Andrew Young
July 2018

Andrew Young served as U.S. Ambassador to the United Nations under President Jimmy Carter, was a two-term mayor of Atlanta, U.S. congressman, and chair of the Centennial Olympic Games hosted in Atlanta in 1996. He is the author of several books, including "Andrew Young and the Making of Modern Atlanta," with Harvey Newman and Andrea Young.

From left: Jay Ward, Felker Ward Jr., South African President Nelson Mandela during Mandela's 1990 visit to Atlanta, Georgia. (Photograph by Bud Smith.)

INTRODUCTION

I've been at this life a long time, 85 years as I write this.

In that time, several things have happened. Number one, I've seen the world turned inside out and upside down, in social, political and governance terms. It's not the same world today as it was 20 years ago, 50 years ago and certainly not 80 years ago.

As a church-going man, a son, a husband, a father of four, a grandfather of five, a retired lieutenant colonel of 20 years, Vietnam combat veteran, lawyer, businessman, Civil Rights proponent and African-American, I have somehow found myself involved in and affected by many of those changes.

I hope that by documenting my life in the pages that follow, others will find it compelling and be motivated to boldly go where others have told them they cannot or should not.

•••

My life is defined by three careers ... and when I find the one that's a perfect fit for me, I'll settle down to it.

The first, after graduating from Tuskegee Institute in May 1953, was a military career, which lasted for 20 years and took me from Atlanta to Texas and Baltimore, as well as to overseas assignments in South Korea, Germany and war-torn Vietnam. I went into the military as a young commissioned officer and retired as a lieutenant colonel more than two decades later.

I have seen the world change from the forced segregation of my childhood in Atlanta and in Alabama, when the color of my skin gave some people license to treat me as being somehow less than they, to adulthood, in which I was named—on two occasions—one of *Georgia Trend*'s "100 Most Influential People in Georgia."

Growing up, most of the people I knew did not have a telephone, or if they did, it was a "party line," so-called because it was shared by multiple families and one never knew who might be listening in.

The media from which we received most of our news was the radio, but again, many people in the neighborhoods where I grew up did not have radios because they did not have electricity.

I recall, as a teenager, seeing my first television set in the window of an appliance store, a 5-inch black-and-white screen housed in a fancy wooden cabinet. People would stand outside the store window and watch the television, even if it offered nothing but a static test signal.

When I think about how far we have come over the last 50 years in the area of communications, I can only conclude that we have lived on two different sides of the communications diaspora—two different sides of the mountain. I dare say that my life, from 1933 until now, represents perhaps the most dramatic—and in some cases, traumatic—transformation in our nation's history. Those things available to us today, whether communications, social interaction or political strength, were unheard of just a few years ago. I consider myself fortunate to have lived in this era of tremendous social change and to have seen both sides.

The Board of Trustees of Tuskegee University meets commencement speaker First Lady Michelle Obama, May 9, 2015. I am sixth from right.

Kindergarten children today are as comfortable with computers as we were with pencils and paper. The day will come when if you mention the word "newspaper," a young person will wonder what you are talking about.

In writing this book, I discovered that when you journey back in time and relive your life—with all its high highs and low lows—all the old joy and hurt come rushing back in equal measure. The good times were those moments you were most proud of. But if a life's accounting is to be worthy, I had to be willing to give a complete account.

At some point along the way, I wondered why I undertook this challenging act in the first place. But by then it was too late, so here goes!

One of several meetings I had with then President Bill Clinton.

I. CHILDHOOD

DETERMINED

From left, the Felker Ward family: Samuel Ward (my uncle, standing), Sarah Lewis (aunt), Azalee Felker Ward (paternal grandmother), Felker Ward Sr. (father, standing), Lewis Ward (paternal grandfather), John Ward (uncle, standing).

1. WHITTIER MILL VILLAGE

My life began on May 4, 1933, when I was delivered at Atlanta's Grady Hospital to Felker W. Ward Sr. and Georgia Ann Ward. I was born in the midst of the Great Depression, the first of three boys. Solomon joined the family three years later; Samuel, 17 years after that.

We lived in the 30-acre Whittier Mill Village in Bolton, Georgia (although the mailing address was Chattahoochee, Georgia); Whittier Mill was a textile factory where cotton was processed and converted to thread for clothing. Mom and Dad both worked at "the mill."

The textile mills in the South of that era built their own residential villages. They didn't pay their employees much, which they mitigated by providing the white workers with homes to live in for little or no rent.

There were more than 100 homes for white families in Whittier Mill Village in the 1940s. J. Slater Baker, who apparently grew up there in the 1940s and '50s, wrote about the village in his autobiography, *The Chattahoochee Boys*. He talked about swimming in Proctor Creek and playing baseball and how the "boys" in the book's title remain friends today.

A March 9, 2015, story in *Atlanta Magazine* by a woman who had lived there since 1983 made Whittier Mill Village sound like the most wonderful place on earth: "Tucked between the Chattahoochee River and Bolton Road south of Vinings ... The area retains much of its late-19th-century charm, and new homes are built to look architecturally similar to the original cottages and bungalows, complete with hipped roofs and front porches ..."

Sounds lovely now, although the story does note that when the mill closed in 1971, "part of the neighborhood was almost made a landfill." The community rebounded, however, and became a National Register Historic District in 1994.

Black employees at Whittier Mill, however, had to fend for themselves in the 1940s; when we lived there, there was only one house on site designated for blacks. In this, the Felker Ward Sr. family was something of an exception.

Our home on the outskirts of the white village had one bedroom, a kitchen and a bathroom. It was situated on one of the largest tracts—one acre—in Whittier Mill Village. Because our house was surrounded by so much open land, it was here that neighborhood games of baseball, marbles and tag were played—with or without me alongside the white children in the community.

We were the only African-American family who lived in the village; everyone else was white. As a child, I always wondered why we lived there. I eventually came to understand the reasons.

There was little mixing between the black and white families at Whittier Mill. We were not social friends, not that way. But they were friendly in a passing acquaintance manner, the way you would be with people you can't avoid seeing day after day. Despite the name-calling, it was not a hostile thing between the white kids and me.

My dad worked as an "office boy" in the management office of the mill. Obviously, he was not a boy, but that was the title. He was always the earliest employee to arrive in the morning because he performed office messenger kinds of work, such as delivering mail to the various desks, starting a morning fire to heat the office in winter, running errands, making coffee and occasionally chauffeuring the top man at the mill, Mr. Julius J. Scott. Mr. Scott had a dark blue, four-door Chrysler with velour interior.

It was, in fact, the most beautiful automobile I had ever seen, and I dreamed of whether or not the day would ever come that *I* would own one like it.

I don't know exactly how much my dad made, but I suspect it was no more than $15 per week. Because of the nature of his work, it was convenient for management that he was close to the village office round-the-clock; that's why we lived where we did.

My mother also worked at the mill. She never finished high school, so her skills were limited. Her principle job was as a sweeper, a job for women to push heavy brooms, sweeping cotton and lint from the weaving machines. She was paid $9 a week in silver dollars, delivered in a small brown envelope. The pay was augmented by free rental on housing.

The working conditions were horrible for my mother, and ladies like her were paid very little. White employees didn't make a lot of money there, either. This was before the days of widespread union organizing, and so it was one step away from slave labor in those textile mills.

My parents did everything they could, I'm sure, to shield my brothers and me from that kind of treatment. Dad was never happy in that job, I'm sure, but it was a job. It was the Great Depression; any kind of job was desirable at that time.

One of the top men at the mill headquarters was Mr. Muse. My grandmother used to wash and iron shirts for Mr. Muse, and she charged him 10 cents for each shirt. It was my duty to pick up the dirty shirts and deliver the clean ones, for which I was paid a total of 10 cents.

Occasionally, when my dad drove Mr. Scott's car, he was allowed to drive it to our home and take our family for a ride. I also recall going to the Scotts' home in Scottdale on a few occasions when my dad had odd jobs to do for the boss. When we were there, our lunch was served at the kitchen table.

Eventually, dad purchased a car for our family. The first was a Ford Model A. At times, the only way he could start the car was with a hand crank in the front, and then he ran around and jumped into the driver's seat before the car took off without him.

•••

In terms of preschool, we didn't have any at Whittier Mill, so my mother prepared me for kindergarten by teaching me to read and do basic arithmetic.

My elementary school education was delivered at Fulton County's segregated William J. Scott Elementary School, a blacks-only, four-room building at the corner of Browntown and Hollywood roads. The first and second grades were in one room, the third and fourth in another, the fifth and sixth in another, and the seventh and eighth were in another.

The teacher of the first and second grades was Ms. Small, the third and fourth grades were taught by Ms. Johnson, and the teacher of the fifth and sixth grades was Ms. Heard. The seventh and eighth grades were taught by Ms. B.M. Andrews; she was also our principal.

In the first- and second-grade room, everyone was exposed to the same daily instruction and work. At the end of my first year, I passed the first- and second-grade examinations and was skipped to the third grade. The same thing happened again the following year and I jumped from the third grade to the fifth grade.

Lunch was free to kids at school, but my parents always gave me a nickel to take with me. Each day that I got that nickel, I saved it for the next day so that, every other school day, I would have a dime, which I used to purchase an RC Cola and a MoonPie, a delicious Southern treat made of graham cracker crust and gooey marshmallow center, cut in the shape of a full moon and dipped in chocolate.

We did not have a playground or playground equipment. For recess, we played marbles or anything else we could think of.

At William J. Scott, I earned all A's, with an occasional B in conduct when I might have been talking when I wasn't supposed to.

"Anybody can get an A in conduct," my dad said. "You don't have to be bright, you don't have to be smart to get an A in conduct."

•••

The village's general store was Shaffer's, owned and operated by Carl Shaffer. Shaffer's sold groceries, toiletries, some clothing, plus odds 'n' ends for use around the house. Families would purchase their groceries on account at Shaffer's, signing an IOU for what their family needed during the week and paying it off on Fridays after payday. This paradigm provided very little opportunity for comparison shopping. You had one place to shop, and that was it.

The store also functioned as the village's post office; the Ward family's post office address was P.O. Box 319, Chattahoochee, Georgia.

My walk to and from Schaffer's took me through the heart of the village. The white kids, many of whom I played games with on our property, would nonetheless yell "Nigger! Nigger!" as I passed their homes. I would not respond until I was headed back toward my house—close enough that I could outrun them to relative safety—and yell back, "Cracker! Cracker!"

They saw no harm in what they were doing. I am sure that these kids were repeating what they had heard in their homes, and I was repeating what I had heard in mine.

These were the same kids who would bring cakes and candy in their dirty little hands to share with me at playtime. My mother and dad would not let me eat any of it.

Our land served many purposes besides residence and community playground. We also raised hogs, chickens and turkeys. Whenever we wanted fried chicken for dinner, Mom or Dad went to the yard, grabbed a young fryer, wrung its neck, dipped it in hot water and plucked its feathers.

Dad was well-liked by the white employees in the office because he served them well, and they got along fine. But everything that happened in those days was absolute segregation. For example, Whittier Mill had its own baseball team and most Saturday afternoons they would play a game against another one of the mills. My dad and I went to the games, but we sat in a blacks-only section of the bleachers. We couldn't sit in the bleachers with Whittier Mill's white employees. My dad was a ballplayer himself, but he wasn't welcome to play on the company team. It was all-white.

•••

My dad was an accomplished hunter, and during hunting season, I went with him. One of our favorite hunting locations was Shorter, Alabama, on land owned by an African-American, Mr. Dave Lewis.

For as long as I can remember my dad always had hunting dogs when I was growing up, something that I would have, too, as an adult.

They were excellent squirrel dogs, and when we took them to the woods, as soon as we shot the first squirrel, the dogs went running off through the swamp to the next tree. It was not unusual for us to kill six or eight in one afternoon.

We also had a good rabbit dog. Tola was a Black and Tan Coonhound that would run rabbits by day, tree possums and coons by night. He was a fine animal. My dad once turned down a $250 offer for Tola, which was a substantial offer in the 1940s.

During the summers when hunting was out of season, my dad, mother, brother Solomon and I would go down to Line Creek for a picnic on our beach "sandbar." We would fish and paddle around in the shallow water. None of us could swim, however, and one day I ventured a bit too far into the currents of the creek and was frightened to death. Dad waded out far enough to grab me and rescue me without us both drowning.

•••

About my dad, Felker Ward Sr.:

When he was in his teens, his father, Lewis Ward, left home. Back in those days, people didn't get divorces. They just left.

The family had a lot of Native American/Indian heritage, including the Creek Nation. Some of it is uncertain now because the Chattahoochee River was once the dividing line between those two tribes. My grandparents on my dad's side ultimately wound up living on the west side of the

My father, Felker Ward Sr.

river.

There were some interesting things to know about dad's family. My grandparents' four children, for example, were all fair-skinned.

My grandmother, Azalee Felker Ward, had three brothers. Two of them lived in Atlanta, the third in Chicago. Azalee was the spine of the family, the one who was always present, always in place while others went off.

Dad, being the oldest boy, had to get a job to help take care of the family—his mother, one older sister, Sarah, and two younger brothers, Samuel and John. But he was determined to get an education. He attended night classes at Atlanta's Booker T. Washington High School and still earned a diploma against all odds and expectations. As you will see later, it was a good thing he did.

I'm not sure what would have become of me had he failed.

My dad particularly loved his middle brother, Samuel. Samuel and his wife, Sis, eventually had 13 children. Samuel had a mechanic's natural instinct. If anything was wrong with a car—or any mechanical device—the neighborhood knew what to do: "Get Samuel; he can fix it."

In addition to being a trusty repairman, Samuel owned his own truck and had a vegetable sales route. He would go to the local farmers market and buy wholesale—tomatoes, beans, cabbage, collards, all that sort of stuff—then drive through the neighborhood with his truck and resell at a fair profit.

The youngest of my father's brothers, John, also worked at Whittier Mill alongside a lot of other folks in the neighborhood. He was most proud of the fact that he was inducted into the Army. John stayed in the service for three years and received an honorable discharge during World War II. That was not the norm; that was something to be proud of during that era. African-American men did not have many opportunities for successful Army careers in those days. Until the day of his death, he was very, very proud of his military record.

John met and married Mary, a girl from West Point, Georgia. She was a beautiful brunette who was so fair-skinned that she almost passed for white. The couple never had any children of their own, so John and Mary were sort of parents to all of us. John, who outlived both of his brothers, was one of the men who followed behind my dad in the church community and he ultimately became the Rev. John Ward.

My grandmother on Dad's side and her brothers had a reputation for never having worked for a company, never having toiled for a white man. They all owned their own businesses. One of Azalee's brothers, Joseph Felker, left the South in the Great Migration for Chicago, Illinois, and started a barber college there. He taught generations of young men the hair trade. He also became a minister.

My paternal grandmother died when I was a teenager. But she quietly acquired roughly 35 acres of land in Cobb County. It was divided among her children when she passed and each inherited about nine acres. Considering that that was during the 1940s and the '50s, it was a priceless inheritance for African-American families to own that much land.

The control that whites had over African-Americans of that era stemmed from the job market. To buy or own property, you needed a decent job. Blacks could not get the better, high-paying jobs. One of the drivers of racism was that the white power structure controlled society by turning poor blacks and poor whites against each other.

Poor whites were the worst. The wealthy whites were not much of a problem for us as we were not a threat to them. It was the poor whites, because they needed somebody to hate and control. I see evidence of that even today, where many still need somebody that they can lord over and dominate. An industrial society encourages this because they maintain their lofty position by having someone else do their dirty deeds for them.

Racism and dealing with racism didn't just happen overnight. It was a gradual move from slavery through Reconstruction.

A lot of young people today would be surprised to know that jobs advertised in newspaper classified section—as late as the 1960s!—were listed "White Only." There were certain jobs listed "For Colored Only." You could not, would not and should not, if you were a black person, waste your time applying for any job advertised as "White Only."

It was not a subtle thing; it was cold reality.

One of the ways that whites consistently suppressed the Civil Rights Movement was through the availability of decent jobs. Following the 1955 Montgomery, Alabama, bus boycott that got the movement started, lots of black people lost their jobs. They were threatened: "If you join this, you're out of work." They had to feed their families, and pay the light bill, etc. It was an economic, disruptive force with which it was hard to reckon.

That position put the greatest burden on smart, educated, upwardly mobile African-Americans who were trying to change things in that era, and at the same time pursue an improved livelihood. It was a real strain on them.

The resistance and ill will engendered out of that was not something that was broadcast loud and clear. You didn't hear about the economic squeeze in three-minute reports on the nightly TV news—if they reported on civil rights actions at all.

Some parents, including my own, strived for their children to receive a good education so they could rise above the suppression that Mom and Dad lived with all their lives.

The greatest influence on my life was my parents. Dad was the most educated ninth-grader I've ever known. And my mother was not a philosopher-type, but she demonstrated her intelligence and grit by what she did day in and day out.

In terms of using whatever money we had, we never went hungry or homeless.

The Great Debate posed by African-American philosophers such as W.E.B. Du Bois and Booker T. Washington was, "What is the way out?" Each espoused a seemingly opposing philosophy. Du Bois, the founder of Atlanta University, felt that intellectual achievement was the way out. Washington, the founder of Tuskegee Institute, took the position, "Cast down your bucket where you are." He emphasized learning a trade and learning how to make things, that doing was the way out.

The ideals were not that far apart if you closely exam their philosophies; they were certainly not as far apart as history has often painted them.

•••

As for my mother, she was a really sweet woman. I could not imagine a better mother than my mother was. She was a good singer. She was loyal to her family, especially to her children.

Mom came from a great family. Back in those days, people like us only married in the "church"—meaning the same denomination. My mother and dad were of the same church affiliation, Church of God in Christ. They took pride all their lives in being good people, uplifting others, and they were deeply supportive of the church and the causes of our community.

My mother grew up in Thomasville, Georgia. Her mother, Mary Jane Simon, was married to Arthur Franklin and they had four boys—David, Malachi, Samuel and Joe—and three girls—Rachel, Annie and my mother. When I first met my grandparents, they were living in Atlanta in a section called Summerhill.

African-Americans lived in clusters around the city. Besides Summerhill, the almost entirely black neighborhoods I remember were Peoplestown, Pittsburgh and Buttermilk Bottom (a.k.a., Buttermilk Bottoms or Black Bottom). We had only two black city high schools in the county, so we got to know a lot of our people all across town.

Arthur Franklin, my mother's father, was a plumber. He always wore a shirt and tie, even when he was doing plumbing work, which could get wet and messy. I never remember seeing him without a coat and tie.

I was around 10 years old when my Grandpapa Arthur died. He and a few other leaders broke away from the church that I describe as "our" church and started one of his own, which also was not unusual in those days. He made himself a bishop in the church. I was told that before he was converted to Evangelical, he was a rough and tough guy. But by the time I knew him, he'd softened his edges and become a leading minister in his church.

The thing I remember about my maternal grandmother was that she loved to fish. Even when she was up in years, after her husband died, everyone knew that someone had to make time at least one day a week to take my grandmother fishing on the Chattahoochee River. Occasionally she would go to one of what we called the "pay" lakes, where you paid two bucks and could fish all day. (I wish that I had had the facility then that I have now, because I own a 17-acre lake in my back yard.) Nothing would have been more wonderful than to have my grandmother there one day a week, every week, sitting on my dock, fishing. She would have felt like she had died and gone to heaven.

Grandpa Franklin knew the Atlanta retail king, Mr. Richard Rich, the founder of Rich's department stores. It was said that my grandfather, if he went to Rich's to buy a pair of socks or whatever and didn't like the price, he would go and find Mr. Rich. Mr. Rich would say, "Well, how much do you want to pay?" Grandpa Franklin would name his own price, and that's what the clerk would mark it down to. I think he must have done some pretty fancy plumbing work for Mr. Rich to earn such royal treatment.

Grandpa Franklin was also unique because he spoke with the accent of his heritage, the Gullah and Geechee. They were people who had emigrated from the West Indies to the barrier islands running along the coasts of Georgia and South Carolina.

Of my mother's siblings, I was closest to the youngest, David, who was only four years older than me. I used to tag along with him. When he went on dates, I was too young to be dating, but I'd go along with him and whomever he was with and hang out.

Grandpa Franklin had a rule that, regardless of what you were out doing, you had to be home by midnight. If you were not home by midnight, you wouldn't get in. The doors were locked; no discussion, no negotiation. One night, David and I didn't make the curfew, so we slept on the porch. Grandpa Franklin was strict about that rule.

Summerhill had once been a majority white community and my grandparents' home was big—it was a three-story house. One of their next-door neighbors was Solomon Walker, an African-American who was the president of Pilgrim Life, an insurance company. The streets in Summerhill were paved and they had sidewalks, two elements missing where my parents lived in Scott's Crossing. The houses in Summerhill were all older, but at some point, it was a high-end community.

My Aunt Rachel was the youngest girl in the family. She often took me to the movies on Saturday afternoons, and we enjoyed popcorn and ice cream cones. That was a real ritual that I looked forward to. (When Rachel died unexpectedly, decades later, unfortunately I was out of town and couldn't easily get back in time for her funeral. That and some other experiences taught me that sometimes you have to re-prioritize, because you might not get a second chance. I have been a leader in the family, the first one on both sides to go to college, and I've been fortunate to have a very successful career. And so I was expected to be there. I still feel badly about having missed her funeral.)

My Uncle Malachi moved to New York, another member of the Great Migration from the South in the 1930s, '40s and '50s. I got a chance to visit him and his wife, Thelma, in New York when I was 20 years old and en route to Germany as an Army second lieutenant. I drove my 1949 Mercury to the Big Apple (and had it shipped to Germany) a few days ahead of my scheduled boat trip across the Atlantic. My first trip to New York City was a great thrill. I'd never seen anything like the tall buildings, the traffic and all the people. It was great preparation for Berlin and the cities I would soon see around the world. Atlanta now is close to what New York was then. It was overwhelming for me going from rural Fulton County to New York.

•••

A few more things you need to know about my mother:

Mom was an outstanding cook. She could take a dollar and feed us on it for a week, or so it seemed.

She was not athletic, yet I distinctly remember being in the yard, playing ball with her, just the two of us.

In terms of meals, she knew that I loved lemon meringue and chocolate meringue pie. But I hated greens, so she declared that I would have to eat my greens before I could get the pie.

She rescued me one time. My dad had gotten himself a pair of beautiful beagle puppies. I was probably 8 years old and I wanted to take the puppies hunting.

I took the two puppies and put them in a culvert in our back yard to go and find a rabbit. The puppies, of course, took off and disappeared into the culvert and wouldn't come out. I was in deep, deep, *deep* trouble. I didn't know what to do, so I ran down to the house and told my mother what I'd done. She got a piece of cooked meat and put it in the culvert so that the puppies could smell it, and she coaxed them out. I don't think she ever told my dad that story.

She was a loving, kind person who did an excellent job of taking care of her family and supporting my dad in whatever he wanted to do.

Mom took great pride in her appearance. Shorts—the food we gave our hogs—were sold in 100-pound cloth bags. The bags had pictures imprinted on them so it was not uncommon in that era for women to make skirts and even whole dresses out of them after the bags were empty.

One thing that did frustrate my dad about my mother was that she never learned how to drive an automobile. Back in those days, we didn't have automatic transmissions. Cars had a clutch and shift levers; they were a mechanical and physical challenge for most men and were almost impossible for many women to master. But Dad tried repeatedly to teach her; I think he believed that it would give her a sense of independence and self-confidence—two characteristics he valued highly. It was the only time I ever saw my dad get impatient with Mom. She would get upset with him and the car, and refuse to do it anymore. She never did master driving, but beyond that, they got along together real well.

In her late 50s, Mom developed breast cancer. She went into remission for a few years, but it returned again, this time fatally, in her early 60s. I don't know that my father ever fully recovered from her loss.

By the time she died, I was a grown man and married to Mary, a woman of whom she not only approved but whom she loved like a daughter and called friend.

•••

When we were old enough to attend school, Solomon and I attended William J. Scott Elementary School on Hollywood Road. To get to the school, we had to walk past a "whites only" school, South Fulton Elementary.

Sometimes, Solomon and I took the short cut, walking along the Southern Railroad Line track to and from school. We tried to avoid being on the railroad when the trains went by because it was frightening, especially when there were "torpedoes"[1] placed on the tracks to serve as signals to the engineers on the train.

It was fun to watch the train pick up and deliver the mail, which was hung on a post next to the rail line. An arm reached out of the train and grabbed an outgoing mailbag as the train sped by; the same conductor would then toss a sack of incoming mail, also without stopping.

Our house was about a hundred yards—the length of a football field—from the railroad tracks. Once we became accustomed to the noise of the passing trains, it was not a bother. In fact, Solomon and I enjoyed counting the train cars as they went by, sometimes seeing as many as 100 in a row.

---

[1] Railroad torpedoes were so named because of the explosive sound the signaling devices made when placed on the tracks. They were intended to signal engineers to stop the train and avoid a potential collision with other trains occupying the same tracks. You can watch a demonstration on YouTube: https://youtu.be/gd3qXHDSWcE .

Solomon was more than a brother to me; he was my companion and, over the years, my very best friend.

There was one black family that lived along the railroad between our house and school. One of their boys was a year or two older than I, and he was quite the bully. Frankly, I was afraid of him, and my younger brother told my mother about the situation.

One afternoon after school, as we approached the bully's house, we spotted our mother, standing along the railroad with a baseball bat in one hand. I don't know exactly what she said to that boy—or what she planned to do with that bat—but whatever it was, she put the fear of God in him and he never bothered us again.

•••

There were times when Solomon and I got a whuppin' for acting up.

On washday, our job was to draw water from a spring at the bottom of a hill near our home. That meant, of course, that we had to walk up the hill carrying full buckets of water, enough for a wash bucket with soap in it and two tubs, one for washing, one for rinsing. We had to carry all that water.

One day I got ornery with my mother.

"I'm tired," I told her. "I'm not going to carry any more water!"

My mother was in the middle of her wash.

"Well, okay," she said, but not as calm as you read the words read here. "When Dad gets home, he's going to take care of you."

Indeed, he came home from work a few hours later and she told him the story. That night, I got the whuppin' of my life. I never talked back to my mother after that day.

•••

Corporal punishment was common in those days, and my sixth-grade teacher, Ms. Heard, had a leather strap with a knot on one end. On one occasion, I came close to being a recipient of that strap.

Walking to school that day, I found an old, discarded pocketknife with a broken blade on the side of the road. I pocketed it and carried it with me to school.

Ms. Heard got wind of it—no doubt after I showed it to my friends— and I lied, denying that I had it. She demanded that I empty out my pockets and it came tumbling out. She sent word for my parents to come down to the school. The knife was absolutely useless, except perhaps to sharpen a pencil, but that didn't matter. I was admonished, but she didn't use the strap on me. It was the fact that I was dishonest that caused my dad the greatest consternation.

"Son," he said, "I don't have any great qualms with you having the knife. But I do have qualms with your not being *honest* about it. You could have easily told the teacher that you used it to sharpen your pencils, which you could do, rather than deny that you had it."

2. LIVING LIFE ON BROWNTOWN ROAD

Dad's resignation from the mill in 1941 to start his own business resulted in our having to leave the relative comfort and familiarity of Whittier Mill Village. He relocated our family nearby into a small, one-bedroom home he and two friends built on the offensively named Browntown Road, in anticipation of the move. Most of the mill's black employees lived in the Browntown Road area.[2]

The Southern Line's tracks were the dividing line between Browntown Road—home to African-Americans—and the nicer neighborhoods of Riverside and Bolton, where only whites could live.

The area in which we moved was known as Scott's Crossing. It was named after the dominant family in the area – the William J. Scott family, for whom the elementary school was also named.

The Scotts' home was at the intersection of Browntown and Hollywood roads. Everyone knew it as a local landmark. There was a general store on the corner that carried limited groceries, but mainly beer, wine, soft drinks and a few other things that were probably not legal. Men gathered on the front porch of Scott's store every evening to drink beer and to discuss and solve the world's problems. As a young boy, oh, how I looked

---

[2] All through the formative years I spent growing up on Browntown Road, I never gave the name a second thought. UNTIL … I was in the Army, far from home, and I had to put down my home address. And I wrote down "Browntown Road." Wait—*Browntown* Road??? That's when it first hit me.

forward to the day when I would be old enough to be invited to sit on the corner with the men!

Scott's Crossing was memorable for its inevitable Friday and Saturday night drunken brawls and, occasionally, a stabbing or a shooting.

In the Browntown Road community, men were mostly laborers and truck drivers, while the women were restaurant workers and domestics. We stood out as the only family in Scott's Crossing that owned a car.

The No. 19 streetcar, called the "River Car," ran along Hollywood Road and stopped at Scott's Crossing. Fares were two tokens for 15 cents. One token would take you in one direction, and the second token brought you back.

I remember the first time I rode on a streetcar. I was with my mother and, as I boarded in front of her, I sat down on the first available seat. After my mother paid the fare, she hurriedly got me up and led me to the back of the car. I did not understand it at the time, but she later explained to me that we could only sit in the back. Even at the young age of 4, the incident left a bitter taste in my mouth.

Nobody on Browntown Road had running water or electricity. Water came from a well and everyone used kerosene lamps for light. The toilet was in the back yard. We had a small coal-burning stove that heated the entire house. My dad would get up in the morning before any of us and make a fire in the stove so we could dress in its warmth. We took our baths in a round stainless steel tub—the same one my mother used for clothes on washday.

The dirt road was poorly maintained. It was then legally outside the city limits of Atlanta, and it was not well kept up by Fulton County. As a result, whenever there was a heavy rain, the road was completely impassible for automobiles. On those occasions, we had to leave our car on Hollywood Road near the streetcar line and my dad would carry me on his back, while my mother carried Solomon from the car line to our house. It is surprising, as I look back today, that nothing ever happened to that car. It was never stolen or vandalized.

The Henry Nellums family lived across the road from us on Browntown Road. My dad and his best friend, Mr. Nellums, played checkers into the wee hours almost every night.

They had a checkerboard they had made themselves, using a 3- by 3-foot piece of plywood on which they painted the squares. They used soda bottle tops as checkers, with one player having his checkers turned up, the other's checkers turned upside down.

It was not uncommon in those days that, as families grew, they would remain rooted in the same general area. Such was the case with us and remains to this day. We still have a number of Wards in the area and the family was eventually recognized by the city of Atlanta, which honored us with Felker Ward Street. It was named after my father and runs off Hollywood Road into the Riverside community.

•••

A few more random thoughts about my father:

Not many people in our community would go on vacation, but my dad usually took our family away for a week to visit relatives in Florida at the end of every school year.

Every Sunday, for example, we spent half of our day in church. Some of our neighbors were there, too; many were not.

My dad was a scoutmaster for Boy Scouts of America Troop 150. At the time, I was too young to be a Boy Scout, but I got all the benefits of it, because I always hung around my dad at the scout meetings.

My dad wasn't much of a hugger; my mother was. But it was always clear that he was very proud of his three sons.

As an adult, I frequently overheard him talking to people about me. It used to embarrass me.

"Dad," I said, "folks don't want to hear all about that—'My son did this, my son did that.' "

But he couldn't help himself, so I gave up trying to dissuade him.

•••

My father was always an entrepreneur at heart.

In 1941, he rented property at 775 Hunter St. (now Dr. Martin Luther King Jr. Drive) and opened a fish and poultry market with live chickens for sale. Customers would come in and pick out the bird they wanted and we would take it to the back room, slaughter and pluck it while the customer waited. We also had fresh fish such as mullet, croaker and, on occasion, Spanish mackerel. When my dad opened his store, we all chipped in and worked there on Fridays and Saturdays, which were our busiest days.

My dad's mother's family's last name was Felker; his father's family's last name was Ward. My dad was given his mother's maiden name as his first name. The men in his family were noted for owning and operating independent businesses. Many of them—most, in fact—took pride in never working for a white man in their life. They had their own businesses—a barber school for this one, a grocery store for another.

•••

We always had a milk cow and a hog that was fattened for slaughter every year.

Hog killing was a big, important winter community event that unfolded for weeks. For most of my childhood, we raised at least one hog for slaughter each year.

When the day arrived, we filled a 55-gallon drum half-full with water and built a fire beneath it.

Mr. J.B. Steed, who lived in nearby Rockdale, was an expert at cleaning and processing hogs. He made appointments for hog killing and made his rounds to our homes on Saturdays. My job was to kill the hog with a .22 rifle, putting a shot right between the eyes. Mr. Steed would arrive just in time to direct the cleaning of the hog. He knew exactly how to quarter and cut up a hog, and he was an expert at dressing the animals. For compensation, each family would give him a cut of the meat.

Hog killing always took place in winter because there was less chance for the meat to spoil. We did not have a smokehouse for curing the meat, so the meat was packed in salt—thus the term salt pork. We also had a hand-operated grinder, which was used for making sausage.

•••

The bulk of our heavy grocery shopping was done on Saturdays on Peters Street, which was near the area that became the Georgia Dome, home of the NFL Atlanta Falcons and the Georgia State University Panthers. There were a series of Jewish-owned stores on Peters Street, which sold food such as rice, meal and sugar in bulk.

My mother always had shopping to do at the five-and-ten stores downtown on Broad Street. At those stores, they baked their own Oreo cookies, and the sweet smell of these baking cookies was a draw for blocks around.

Shopping was often the highlight of our week (if we weren't hunting or fishing or playing ball). Our shoes were bought at the Thom McAn store; I remember trying on a pair of white and brown saddle oxfords. They were too small for my feet, but the store did not have my correct size in stock. I wanted those shoes so much, I pretended they didn't hurt, even though they were killing me. My mother and dad bought the shoes for me and I suffered in them in silence for months until it became clear to me my feet were never going to get smaller.

Our first home electric icebox was manufactured by Frigidaire. We referred to it not as an icebox or refrigerator but as our Frigidaire, the same way "the Xerox machine" later became generic for copiers and tissues were all "Kleenex."

3. THE MOVE TO TUSKEGEE

Following the Japanese attack on Pearl Harbor on Dec. 7, 1941, there was a sharp buildup in U.S. Armed Forces to fight the ever-expanding war overseas. Many military leaders said there was untapped talent available.

And for the first time, the War Department experimented with enlisting African-American men to be trained as fighter pilots. There was great consternation and doubt in Washington, D.C., about the viability of this endeavor, but military officials pushed forward. The need for fresh bodies to be thrown against the Axis powers was more important than traditional social mores separating black- and white-skinned Americans. The democracy governing men and women and children of all skin colors was under attack. The decision was made to house the program in the Tuskegee area.

Mrs. Eleanor Roosevelt, President Franklin Delano Roosevelt's wife, visited Tuskegee herself and volunteered to take a flight with an African-American pilot trainee. The Secret Service and all other authorities did their best to discourage her, but Mrs. Roosevelt was a headstrong First Lady who did what she wanted and she took a flight over their objections. This public act of civil disobedience bolstered the program and flight training was officially ordered to go forward on the grounds of Tuskegee Institute.

At Tuskegee Institute, a historically black college in Macon County, Alabama, aviation cadets were given ground school training on the school's campus and received their primary flight training at Moton Field[3],

---

[3] It was named after Dr. Robert Moton, the second president of the college.

just outside of the city. The War Department subsequently constructed a larger base for advanced training, about 10 miles west of Tuskegee, and it served as home base for the Army Air Corps units later known as the Tuskegee Airmen. If you've seen the movie *Red Tails*, the plane they fly was the plane that the Tuskegee Airmen flew out of their base.

There was great resistance to this program in Washington—and locally, where white skeptics doubted that black men could be trained to fly airplanes.

(Macon County had no shortage of whites who feared what would happen if an entire generation of educated, young black men and women and their families took hold of Tuskegee.)

The arrival of pilot candidates and airplanes created another immediate need: African-American mechanics who could maintain the fleet. (The War Department figured it would be easier to train black men to maintain planes for black pilots than to expect white men to do it. In those days, that was probably the right call.)

A wide net was spread across Georgia, Alabama, Mississippi, Florida, Tennessee, Texas and South Carolina for candidates to be trained as aircraft mechanics at Tuskegee. The main requirement was that they have a high school education. My dad had that and volunteered for this new defense job, closing his fish and poultry business.

Mechanics trained on the AT-6 aircraft on which the cadet pilot training took place. Thousands of men eventually completed this course and earned high-paying jobs—high compared with what someone like my dad could earn as an "office boy."

After basic training on the AT-6, the new pilots and their mechanics advanced to fighter aircraft—P-51s and P-38s.

The benefits to black culture that resulted from this experiment are almost indescribable. A generation that had, theretofore, been relegated to manual and menial labor saw the world in a whole new way.

This is an aspect of the Tuskegee Airmen story that has been largely overlooked by the history books. Job opportunities available at the time were slim; even college-educated black men were limited at the high end of the career spectrum to being schoolteachers, federal postal workers, social workers or bus drivers. A whole new atmosphere resulted from my dad and a thousand others like him, who finally had an opportunity to earn a decent living—and living condition—for their families.

The only jobs that people who looked like my dad and me could apply for at that time were those segregated by color. It didn't matter how much education you had; there was a limit for what you would be considered a candidate.

The circumstances in which black men functioned in that era tended to downgrade their manhood.

There's an old saying that "Necessity is the mother of invention." That was indeed the case during World War II.

There was a strong resistance to it. The belief among many whites was it just would not work. And that was just a part of the pushback. The other part was the fact that the government was taking this sub-class that it had spent its entire history suppressing, mentally and physically, and moving them up a notch. Poor whites would no longer have anyone under them on the social ladder.

Tuskegee was chosen in part because it had a pretty low cost of living, as well as the availability of a better educational climate. In that environment, military pay would qualify you to be middle class.

•••

African-American men who were heads of household found themselves with responsible jobs, making good money, able to provide a middle-class way of life for their families.

The atmosphere in our family's home was greatly enhanced by this development. Programs such as the one that created the legendary Tuskegee Airmen resulted in a whole new class of family life—and expectations—for African-Americans.

The Tuskegee city fathers feared there would be an explosion of affluent, successful African-Americans in their city who would expect and demand equal treatment at banks, clothing stores, recreation facilities, theaters and so on. In some cases, they actually closed these businesses rather than allow their integration and utilization by African-Americans.

Black entrepreneurs, newly enriched and empowered by the government, got around this whites-only behavior by creating all kinds of businesses of their own, black-owned, black-supported and, most important, black-rewarded.

The pride that I took in seeing these developments laid the groundwork for my decision later in life to become a military pilot. When I attended flight school, some 14 years later at Fort Rucker, Alabama, I was taught by some of the very same instructors who were teachers for the original Tuskegee Airmen.

•••

Mechanics' training was done on the Tuskegee Institute campus. Dad went there without us for approximately three months, and as soon as he completed his training, he uprooted our family again, this time to Tuskegee, Alabama.

The move to Tuskegee brought a completely new way of life—and living—to the Ward family.

First of all, we lived in a "project," a new, government-built apartment complex comprised of three-bedroom units, complete with kitchen and bath with hot and cold running water—upscale living conditions compared with what we came from in Scott's Crossing.

My brother and I had separate bedrooms for the first time. As a family, we were able to shop and be entertained in the Alabama cities of Auburn and Opelika.

Dad purchased a 1938 Chevrolet and when the engine ultimately quit, he and I took it apart, piece by piece, and rebuilt it. He taught me how engines function, and that knowledge helped me throughout my life.

The housing projects were on Franklin Road, near the entrance to Tuskegee Institute. As a result, my brother Solomon and I only had to walk a block to school at the Chambliss Children's House, a laboratory school on the Tuskegee Institute campus.

My grades fell off a cliff when we moved from Atlanta to Tuskegee, from A's to C's. It soon became evident that there were serious flaws in the education I had received at William J. Scott Elementary back in Atlanta.

It took us a while to figure out what was going on: The educational standards—and expectation—were so much higher at Tuskegee than they had been in Fulton County. Discovering this caused an initial shock to my parents—and me—and it took a while to acclimate and catch up. My mother and father, who had come up in the Fulton County system, were not much help to me at this point. It took a year, but I caught up in a big way, performing on par or above the other students at Chambliss. By the time I was in the eighth grade, I was once more an A student.

•••

In the ninth grade, I entered a public speaking contest sponsored by the New Farmers of America (NFA). The organization was created in Tuskegee in 1935 and soon became a national black youth counterpart to the Future Farmers of America (FFA), started seven years earlier in Kansas City, Missouri. My English teacher, Miss Johnson, stayed after school and rehearsed my speech with me practically every day in preparation to deliver my speech, "Strength for the Task Ahead." (I enjoyed this in no small part because I had a crush on Miss Johnson. Of course, if she knew, she never acknowledged it.)

I won first place in the countywide competition and triumphed again at the state level. That earned me the chance to compete in the regional contest at North Carolina A&T College.

For this occasion, I needed a suit—something I did not own. My mother and father put the money together and took me to Auburn, where I picked out a brown tweed. (I wore it for years until I finally outgrew it.) I finished second in the regionals. I was still quite young and was embarrassed when my voice cracked as I gave my speech.

•••

Chambliss Children's House was a school with a mix of traditional teachers and Tuskegee Institute students studying to be teachers.

Back in Fulton County, the only reason African-American children received any education at all was because the *federal* government required it. Whites in Atlanta were not real eager—or motivated—to have educated blacks coming up through the system and questioning their continued place at the bottom of society. As such, the state of Georgia provided the bare minimum education possible. (I saw that in high school a few years later, when my family returned to Atlanta.) Black students never had enough textbooks to go around and the ones we had were worn-out, out-of-date editions handed down from the white high schools. Even our football uniforms were hand-me-downs from the white schools.

But in Tuskegee, under the aegis of the Institute and a well-educated, African-American upper middle class, there was a different attitude. Parents of my classmates at the Children's House were aircraft mechanics, college professors, even pilots. They wanted their kids to be smarter and they knew that, given the same opportunities, their sons and daughters were just as smart as the white kids.

•••

I still remember a little something about several of my classmates at Chambliss Children's House:

• Inez Hastings had the highest grade point average.

• Jewett Reynolds went on to high school at Palmer Memorial Institute in Sedalia, North Carolina, and then Fisk University.

• Pee Wee and Tiny were fraternal twins.

• George Howell, who had a successful career in the Air Force, settled back in Tuskegee, where he lived the rest of his life. He did a great service of keeping us in touch after we finished school and many of us had moved on.

• Louis Exam's father had a service station on Franklin Road right beside the campus.

• William Anderson was the best athlete of us all, and I often wondered whatever happened to him. I am sure he was good enough to make a college football team if he ever got the opportunity.

I especially remember a day in ninth grade when an AT-6 had engine problems and had to make an emergency landing in the school pasture adjacent to Franklin Road. All of the boys from our high school took off running after the airplane and arrived there before any Army officials did. The plane was not damaged, and men like my father ultimately repaired it onsite and it flew back to the base.

My interest in flying was born in those Tuskegee days, and I knew that someday I would fly just like the pioneering Airmen did.

•••

When we moved to Tuskegee, my first entrepreneurial exploit was as a shoeshine boy. The Chambliss Children's House had a woodworking shop and I made a box to hold my shoe polish, brushes and rags. I set up for business on the Tuskegee campus, where students would sit on the wall beside the administration building and place their feet on the box, and I shined their shoes for 10 cents per shine.

After that, I went down to the neighborhood Piggly Wiggly store and asked for a job.

I was hired to bag groceries and take them to our customers' cars. The biggest tip I received was 25 cents. It also fell to me to clean the employee washroom. I scrubbed the washbasin and mopped the floors, but did not clean the commode. The manager saw what I'd done—and what I had not—and decided to show me exactly how it was to be done: he cleaned the toilet with his bare hands. *His bare hands!* After that experience, I quit! I would not clean a toilet with my hands.

Next up I took over a newspaper route, which I delivered every morning on my bicycle before class.

Many homes in Tuskegee at that time still did not have electricity. But they did have iceboxes and that inspired a new business venture for me: delivering ice to the neighborhood.

Mr. Slim Morgan lived near our house. I made a deal with Mr. Morgan to use his horse and wagon for peddling blocks of ice around the Greenwood community: We split my profits 50/50. The only icehouse around was on the edge of town, and I would drive the horse and wagon there daily and buy a 100-pound block of ice, scored into four 25-pound blocks. The ice cost me a penny per pound and I re-sold it for 2 cents a pound, a 100 percent profit. My parents encouraged my entrepreneurship, buying me a small bell, and I drove through the village, ringing my bell and hollering, "Ice man! Ice man!" I had a regular route, and my customers depended on my coming through twice a week to supply their ice needs.

Many homes in the area had wood stoves for cooking and I hatched another idea. I went to the nearest sawmill and they let me haul away, free of charge, all of the slabs that the horse and wagon could carry.[4] I made an even higher profit on this because my material cost for this wood was zero.

•••

In my youth, I used to hunt rabbits with my dad. When I was 10, he

---

[4] Slabs are the edges containing bark, trimmed away to prepare trees for cutting or sawing into lumber for building.

gave me my first shotgun, a single-shot 410 with a .22 rifle on top. Any Saturday afternoon in the fall and winter, you could always find my dad and me hunting together, sometimes with another one of his friends. In the summertime, the whole family went fishing together on Saturday afternoons.

Another thing I got to do pretty young thanks to my dad's faith in me? Driving.

The roads in and around Tuskegee were dirt, and not well-maintained or often traveled. As a result, when I was 13, Dad let me sit on his lap and steer our car around. By the time I was 14, I had my driver's license. (They did not require birth certificates back in those days.)

•••

At the height of World War II, my dad rose to maintenance crew chief. Part of his job was to not only maintain airplanes, but to test-fly them with pilots, which gave the mechanics incentive to make sure they did everything right.

•••

My parents were probably the happiest when they lived in Tuskegee. They made real friends in Tuskegee, with couples who were like them, hard-working, ambitious, interested in the outside world.

While we were at Tuskegee, my dad entered the ministry. Church leadership then was not based on seminary training; it was a matter of the character of the man, and his ability to read the Bible and articulate and share in a meaningful way what he read. My dad could do all of that, so he wound up being selected as a pastor.

He started by pastoring a group of approximately 10 people in Tuskegee. When we moved back to Atlanta after the war, the church occupied a growing amount of Dad's time. He became known to all as "Reverend Ward." That was the way of life for our family: community leadership, doing what's right and always reaching upward. Over the years he rose to district superintendent, which meant that he had three or four churches under his jurisdiction.

We never had alcohol in our household, with one exception. One day I found a half-pint bottle of liquor in the house. I couldn't figure out why it was there. My parents never drank it. I later learned what it was for. In those days, when you had a cold, the home remedy was to sweat it out of you. They boiled green pine needles and lemon and poured a little bit of the bourbon in it. That half-pint of liquor would last a whole year in our house. Another home remedy was to take a dose of castor oil and a teaspoon of sugar with a few drops of turpentine. Those remedies were so undesirable that you would have to be one step away from death to admit that you had a cold.

4. BACK TO ATLANTA

I did not realize until years later what a blow the end of World War II was to the Tuskegee economy and to its families, mine included.

On July 26, 1948, President Harry S. Truman issued Executive Order 9981 directing the integration of the U.S. Armed Forces. The order stated that "It is hereby declared to be the policy of the President that there shall be equality of treatment and opportunity for all persons in the armed services without regard to race, color, religion, or national origin." The order also established the President's Committee on Equality of Treatment and Opportunity in the Armed Services (Fahy Committee).[5]

The noble Tuskegee Airmen experiment was a wartime success. When the war ended, the Tuskegee military base was shut down. The decision to close the Army Air Corps base at Tuskegee was also done to cut down the overall number of bases being maintained in peacetime.

When the base closed in 1948, almost overnight there were no jobs for men like my dad. Some of them moved back where they'd come from or to new places. We stayed on for a year, and my dad was reduced to performing odd jobs for considerably less pay. When the government literally closed the Tuskegee Army Airfield, it disassembled all those barracks and my dad and I took jobs with a contractor, tearing down buildings and driving nails out of boards.

Dad also worked with an electrician who taught him how to wire houses.

Eventually, however, opportunities dried up in Tuskegee, the friends we made during the war years moved away, and Dad had no choice but to

---

[5] Source: https://www.trumanlibrary.org/anniversaries/desegblurb.htm

pack us up and move us back to Atlanta where we had family, a support system and the vague hope that his new skills could lead to a better life.

•••

In reality, life was very different for my dad after we left Tuskegee. He had become accustomed to being well-paid, to having achieved a level of prestige for his station in life and to being treated with respect.

There was none of that easily found back in Atlanta.

Upon our return to Atlanta, Dad took his credentials and applied to Delta Air Lines for a mechanic's job. The foreman looked at his paperwork, acknowledged that, indeed, he had the requisite training and experience for a mechanic's job. However, he informed my dad, he could not hire him in that capacity because if he did, every white mechanic on the line would walk off the job.

After Delta turned him down, he took up the business of tearing down dilapidated houses. He was allowed to salvage whatever lumber and bricks that he could and resell them. That's what he did to bring in income to the family for about a year until he landed a decent job with the General Services Administration (GSA), where he put his skills back to work in wheeled-vehicle mechanics.

He stayed with the federal government for the next 15 years until his retirement in 1967.

•••

The house that Dad built before we moved to Tuskegee was rented out and earned us income, so it was some time before we were able to relocate its tenants and move back in. In the interim, we stayed in Uncle Gwette's house in Cobb County. After our Tuskegee years, the house was three steps backward: no running water—not even a well—or electricity. Every washday, Solomon and I went back down to the spring, carrying back countless buckets of water.

For entertainment, we went out to the car and turned on the radio and listened to whatever program desired. We always caught the fights when Joe Louis, "The Brown Bomber," was featured.

When Dad built the house, it consisted of just one room: a combination of bedroom, sleeping room, sitting room and kitchen with an outdoor toilet. The county finally ran electricity, water and sewer lines down Browntown Road, so Dad built another room on it, this time adding an indoor toilet as well. Then we were in tall cotton: We had two bedrooms!

Once we had a home outfitted with electricity again, Dad brought home a new RCA Victor radio. We looked forward to "The Lone Ranger" every week. It was part of our routine. We also listened to "Fibber McGee and Molly" and "The Aldrich Family."

I'll give you a good example of how human nature works. When I was a kid, the main radio station in Georgia was WSB. It was a powerful station. Back then, stations went off the air at night; few were on 24 hours a day. WSB shut down every night to the tune of "Dixie." Nobody talked much about it; there was no uprising over it. We all sang "Dixie." Segregation and discrimination—there was nothing we could do about it. The kinds of things that our young people were able to accomplish later on by sit-ins and the Civil Rights Movement, none of that went on when I was a child. You adjusted to it; it became part of your DNA.

•••

My first cousin Miriam "Mae" Ward Culver is the daughter of my Uncle Samuel, my father's brother.

Mae—who had 12 brothers and sisters—is 11 years younger than I and one of the last people in my family to still call me "Billy." Why Billy? Because when I was growing up, my dad was Felker to everyone in the family. Rather than call me "Junior," the family used my middle name, William, and called me Billy.

Nicknames have always been more commonly used in my family than given names.

Growing up, I was closer to Mae's older sister, Barbara, but as we have aged, Mae and I have gotten to know each other better. There were so many cousins in our family that we tended to behave more like brothers and sisters. We were always there for each other, in good times and bad.

"We were taught that that was not just your cousin, that was your brother," Mae said. "And we looked at the older ones with respect, because they had to help with the younger ones. They had to help raise the younger ones."

Once I joined the service and became a pilot, Mae remembered that I would occasionally give the cousins a thrill when I was home for a few days.

"Billy would tell us he was going to fly over our house on the last day of his leave and do a little wing flying—you know, he'd wave at us with the wing," she said. "Everybody would go outside where we could see him. We'd know that it was him, because he'd come down low and tilt his wing to let us know that he loved everybody. That was very, very exciting as a child.

"Billy helped a lot with my younger sisters and brothers," Mae recalled, "as far as mapping a direction they should go in life.

"Sammy was Billy's younger brother, but Sammy was more like his son," Mae said, and it was true. "Billy was 20 years older than Sammy. He was about that much older than my youngest sister Suzanne, too. They had to do what he'd tell them to do. They were trained to do what the older ones told them to do without any question, because we knew that they were not going to steer us in the wrong direction. Because if they did, then they had to answer to our uncles and my dad. They didn't take any mess.

"We were very proud of Billy. My younger brother, Grady, went into military service on Billy's recommendation. Unfortunately, he got sick while serving and Billy, with his position, helped guide him, making sure that he went to the right doctors.

"Whenever we needed something, we called Billy. He would jump on it to make sure that everything was going like it should. He helped the family a lot. Being a lawyer, with all his contacts, he was a big help. He helped take care of my uncle and my other Aunt Mary, financially, when they had hard times.

"But it wasn't just Billy helping raise and support all of us kids.

"Billy's father, my Uncle Felker, took my youngest sister, Suzanne, to her prom when Daddy couldn't go. His next-door neighbor threw a party for the seniors after the prom. And my dad told her, 'Well, since the party is next door to your Uncle Felker, you can go.' She thought, 'Great, I'm loose!' Suzanne did not realize that Uncle Felker was going to sit right there. She said that was the most terrible time! She tried to get him to leave, and he would not! She was so embarrassed because when one of the boys started talking to her, he'd question him: 'What's your name? Who are your parents?' She wanted to just drop in a hole, because that was so embarrassing. They thought they were helping. That's all I can say; they thought they were helping. Thank God it was her and not me!

"We cousins never did get away too much with anything," Mae said. "There were too many relatives in the area. I don't know whether that was good or bad!"

5. DAVID T. HOWARD HIGH SCHOOL

Ienrolled at David T. Howard High School in Atlanta as a sophomore. At that time, there were two high schools for African-Americans in the city, Howard on the east side of town and Booker T.
Washington High School on the west side.

There was a residency requirement to determine which boys
and girls would attend which school. Officially, we lived on the west side,
so I would technically be assigned to Washington High. My dad, however,
was a friend of Mr. Charles L. Gideons, the principal at Howard, and that
was where my dad wanted me to attend. We did what was often done in
those days: We used my grandparents' address on the east side to finesse
enrollment at Howard.

While I was attending Howard, an Explorer Boy Scout troop was
formed, led by our English teacher, Mr. John Wesley Miles. It was there
that I met lifelong friends such as Herman J. Russell, William Kimbrough,
Vernon Jordan (future friend and adviser to President Bill Clinton) and
A.D. King, the younger brother of Martin Luther King Jr. While I had not
previously been a Boy Scout, I had unofficial training because my dad was
the scoutmaster of Troop 150 when I was a kid, and I accompanied him
and the rest of the scouts in all of their camping programs. When Mr. Miles
did not have a place for the Explorers to camp, my family gave the troop
permission to camp on my late grandmother's property on Queen Mill
Road in Cobb County.

My history teacher at Howard was Mr. Marcus "Pop" Beavers. Mr.
Beavers felt that comprehension and mastery of the English language was
far more important to us as young African-Americans than was history.
He, therefore, taught us a second, broader swath of English, not history.
The result was that we had two English teachers.

•••

My first girlfriend was when I was 14 and in the 10th grade at Howard. Her name was Ruby Hart and she was a beautiful girl, a little bit older than I was, and certainly more mature.

Her family lived in one of Atlanta's downtown housing projects. I'd walk her home from school, carrying her books, whenever I could. The only place we could sit and be together at her house was on the porch, because they didn't have a sitting room as such. They had one bedroom and I certainly wasn't allowed in there with her. We didn't have much money, so our most exciting dates were going to an occasional movie at the Strand Theater.

I don't remember any great break-up. We didn't have much means of communication, other than school. When we were no longer at the same school—I transferred from Howard to Booker T. Washington High School—I never went back across town to visit with Ruby.

•••

Herman J. Russell lived in Summerhill at the corner of Little and Love streets, one block from where my grandparents on my mother's side lived, at the corner of Frazier and Little. As a 14-year-old kid, I enjoyed the city life and hung out with Herman and his friends whenever I could. We got to know each other well and eventually would be college roommates, business partners and lifelong friends.

Herman was an endless source of fascination and inspiration. He had a stubborn speech impediment that made understanding him a challenge for passing acquaintances, but it was no big deal for his friends and family.

He was also a teenager with an unrepentant entrepreneurial streak.

While we were in high school, Herman owned and operated a hamburger joint on Auburn Avenue. When everyone else was out playing on Saturday afternoons, Herman was flipping hamburgers and making money.

The two of us also worked for Herman's dad every summer. Rogers Russell was a plasterer and he paid us to do construction work for him. We pushed wheelbarrows full of mud, as we called it, for bricklaying, block laying or plastering for small commercial buildings.

We didn't get rich, but I had money to buy clothing or, if I went on dates, I had my own money to spend. (My dad always taught me that, if I was living at home, no matter what age I was, to share some of my earnings with my mother. He said, "You ought to show your appreciation for your mother washing your clothes and cooking your food and everything else. Give her some of what you earned," and I did that. That was an important part of my upbringing.)

Herman was not a musician, but he organized and managed a

successful jazz band. He couldn't read a single note of music or play a musical instrument. But by God, he had this band: Columbus "Duke" Pearson on piano, "Silly Willie" Wilson on trombone, Aaron Cook on trumpet, and David Hudson on clarinet. They rehearsed in the basement of his parents' house in Summerhill and I was often on hand to listen and cheer them on.[6]

(I had my own music dreams for a time; my Uncle David—my mother's youngest brother—had an alto saxophone. He no longer played, so rather than let it gather dust, he let me have it. I took lessons and played in the David T. Howard High School band. That went fine until my uncle took back his horn and pawned it. My mother and dad didn't have the money to get me another one, so that ended my musical career.)

Herman always called me "Doc."

The reason for that, he said, was "You're the only one out of our group that was smart enough."

The black schools didn't have facilities back in those days for advanced children, so they would skip you. I skipped two grades in elementary school, which was how I caught up to Herman, grade-wise, despite him being two years older.

•••

My inspiration to do well and try to be a good person was reflective of my father and mother's lives and the inspiration that they provided to my brothers and me. My dad had a philosophy. He told us, "Do not look up to any man and don't look down on any man. Look them all straight in the eyes."

I remember one Sunday, my dad and I were on the way to church. He was pastor of a church in Ellenwood, Georgia. We came upon a man on a corner of Decatur Street who seemed to be drunk.

I said, "It's a shame this guy is drunk on Sunday morning."

"Son, we're can't be sure that he's drunk."

For whatever reason, Dad stopped the car and we walked over to the man. As it turned out, my dad's instincts were sharp: the man suffered from epilepsy and was having an epileptic fit. Dad did what he could to calm and comfort the man until an ambulance arrived.

---

[6] In his own memoir, *Building Atlanta: How I Broke Through Segregation to Launch a Business Empire* (Chicago Review Press, 2014), Herman updated the band's later careers: "Duke Pearson became a producer and arranger at Blue Note Records (and) led his own band, the Duke Pearson Orchestra, and played with Donald Byrd, Art Farmer, and Chick Correa, as well as vocalists Nancy Wilson, Carmen McRae, and Joe Williams. Willie Wilson played with Dizzy Gillespie."

That was the kind of man my father was; I've always remembered those simple acts of human kindness. In my life, I attempted to pass the same approach on to my children. That is, don't be so quick to judge. Things are not always the way they might seem on the surface. Whenever issues come up within the family or among my friends or the greater community, I'm usually the last one to express an opinion, because I like to hear all the details before I do.

My dad was a very smart man and I was very fortunate to have him in my life for as long as I did.

6. FELKER WARD JR., TOBACCO FARMER

In 1948, I signed up to join a group of teenage boys who were hired to work each summer on tobacco farms in Connecticut. Few people realize that—in those days—more tobacco was raised in Connecticut than in North Carolina.

There were not many summer jobs available for black high school boys in Atlanta, so I was anxious for this opportunity. Mr. "Pop" Beavers—the history/English teacher at Howard—helped arrange and dole out the jobs each year.

In late May, a group of boys gathered on the Morehouse College campus to depart for Connecticut. We had tickets on the Silver Comet train that left Atlanta's Terminal Station at 7:05 in the evening. It was an all-night train ride to Washington, D.C. When we arrived in the nation's capital, we were directed to exit the train and then re-board. Why? Because we had been segregated from Atlanta to Washington in a "Blacks Only" car. When we re-boarded, we were instructed to sit anywhere that we wished for continuing the trip on up to New York. This was my first brush with integration.

The minimum age for the tobacco farming program was 16 because if you worked in the program, you worked 10-hour days. All of the boys were 16—except me. I was only 15. I convinced Pop Beavers that I not only wanted to go but that I needed to go. He told me to go ahead and board the train as scheduled, and inform the employers at L.B. Haas & Co., the tobacco company where we would work, that Pop had my birth certificate. (Of course, he did not.)

Things went quite well for the first few weeks until the Haas employment office wrote to the state of Georgia and obtained a copy of my birth certificate. We were working 12 hours a day, and it was against the law in

Connecticut for anyone under the age of 16 to work more than eight hours a day. Instead of sending me home, they decided to let me stay and work eight hours a day then return to the barracks for the rest of the day. Needless to say, this was embarrassing to me, and all of the other boys kidded me about my youth.

"Young blood, if—when we come back here in the afternoon—you've used up all the hot water, you're going to be in trouble, physically."

I made sure I didn't.

While on the tobacco farm, we lived in former World War II Army barracks, took turns at KP and worked hard in the fields. The tobacco grown in Connecticut was cigar tobacco, which was grown in "bents." Bents were sections of the fields that were divided by upright poles, approximately 20 feet apart, and 10 feet in height. The fields were covered with netting, which was rolled up during the day, and down at night, to maintain a somewhat constant temperature within the extremely large growing fields.

At the time we arrived, the small tobacco plants were in beds. Our first chore was to replant them in the fields. Approximately three weeks after replanting, we hoed the fields to remove weeds and suckers, which were sprouts that developed between the leaves and the main stem of the tobacco plant.

Next came the harvesting of the tobacco. I was lucky enough to be assigned to work in the "sheds," where there were teenage girls assigned to string the tobacco leaves onto wooden lathes for hanging and curing. It was much cooler in the sheds and a much better working environment than in the fields.

Most of the other boys were accustomed to drinking alcohol. I, on the other hand, had never had a sip in my life. Not wanting to be left out, I bought a bottle of Mogen David MD 20/20 one Saturday. The taste was so good that, over the period of the afternoon, I drank the whole bottle. I woke up the next day with an indescribable headache and hangover. How bad was it? I would have had to get better to die. It was not until Monday that I finally began to feel alive again, and I chose to not have another drink of any kind of alcohol—especially not the one known as "Mad Dog 20/20."

The tobacco farm experience was a great one for me, in that I was able to be on my own, away from home all summer, and yet not unsupervised. (It probably eased my transition to college less than two years later and the Army after that.)

Pop Beavers was there to supervise us. There was also a medical student, Dr. C. Clayton Powell—he later became a prominent physician in Atlanta—and a doctoral student who was studying at Harvard University. The doctoral student, whose name, unfortunately, I cannot recall, was also a musician and, for the summer, we formed a chorus on the farm. We performed at a nearby church on Sundays. We had a great time and were always well-received.

To help pass my time off, I often hitchhiked a ride from Hazardville, Connecticut, where we worked, to Springfield, Massachusetts.

Hitching a ride was quite easy in those days. On one trip, a married couple gave me a ride and invited me to their home for dinner. I gladly accepted, and after dinner, they took me back to the farm. I was privileged to be invited back several times that summer. They were curious to know about Tuskegee and conditions in the South in general, as they had read about George Washington Carver and Booker T. Washington but wanted first-hand information.

I saved my earnings while on the tobacco farm and sent the money home regularly to my mother and dad, who set it aside for me for my future. It was a memorable experience, and one that I will always fondly recall.

7. BOOKER T. WASHINGTON HIGH SCHOOL

Having spent much of elementary school and my freshman year of high school in Tuskegee, sophomore year at David T. Howard High School in Atlanta did not challenge me much.

The city of Atlanta school board opened a third high school for African-Americans that year that it called Carver Vocational School. Carver was designed as an alternative for kids with vocational—as opposed to academic—skills. I always enjoyed test-taking to determine my talents and volunteered to take the test for possible enrollment at Carver. The results came back positive, and I was ordered to attend Carver.

To say that I was absolutely horrified would be an understatement. I didn't dare tell my parents what I had done.

As luck would have it, two weeks into my attendance at Carver, my dad ran into Principal Gideons downtown. He asked my dad why he had taken me out of his school.

Dad was shocked to say the least. He quickly realized that Carver was not the best place for me and applied to the school board to have me reinstated in regular high school. The superintendent, Ira Jarrell, directed that I take a battery of tests to determine exactly where I should matriculate.

I did well on those tests, scoring at the college sophomore level in English—and college freshman level in math—even though I was only in the 10th grade.

Dad and I were ordered to a meeting at the superintendent's office on a Saturday morning to hear the verdict in person. Jarrell reviewed my test grades and agreed that I should be in a regular academic high school.

He added, in words that I found offensive, "Based on your test scores, Felker, if you do not make all A's in school, you should have your ass whipped."

In the course of writing out the order sending me back to Howard, he asked for our address.

My dad, in his glee and excitement, forgot about the east side/west side divide, forgot that my official school registration was at my grandparents' home in Summerhill, to the east, and mistakenly gave Superintendent Jarrell our correct home address on the west side of town.

If you're keeping score, I attended Tuskegee Institute High as a freshman and David T. Howard High as a sophomore. At the start of my junior year, I wound up at my third high school, Carver High (for two weeks), followed by my fourth, Booker T. Washington High. I often tell people that I was a constant troublemaker, and that I was moved from school to school. Of course, that was not the case, but it made for a better story.

The good news was that I completed my junior and senior years at the same time and graduated high school in three years.

8. GOD CAME TO ME DISGUISED
AS A WATER MOCCASIN

We all, eventually, come to a point where we must choose to enjoy life. We can't walk around full of hate—on the surface, at least.

You've probably heard the expression, "I knew my place." If we are successful, we become people who know our place in the world. That's the way it was with me at a certain age.

But at the same time, I was a human being who realized my "place" in society—at least according to the white establishment—was not right. I knew that I had to find the opportunities to make my own place in the world.

I had to choose my spot to stake a claim.

•••

One Sunday afternoon when I was a young boy, my dad was driving my mother, my brother Solomon and me up Atlanta's Bankhead Highway (later renamed Donald Lee Hollowell Parkway). Dad was pulled over for speeding, 40 or 50 miles per hour, I suppose, in a 35 mile per hour zone.

Two police officers came up from behind our car, one on each side, and they executed the good cop/bad cop routine we've all seen on television and in movies.

The bad cop was an overweight redneck with a great big belly. He said, "Boy, where do you think you are going?"

"I am going to church, officer," my dad said.

"No you are not," the redneck cop said. "You are going to jail for speeding."

There was a slight dent on the fender of my dad's car, and the bad cop assumed it was because of dad's "fast driving" that the car had been damaged.

My dad tried telling him the truth, that the car was parked in a lot when the damage was done by an unknown vehicle.

The redneck cop fired back, "It's no wonder, as fast as you drive, nobody could catch you to damage your car." I'm still not sure how he thought that even made sense.

After 10 or 15 minutes of continued verbal abuse and attempts at humiliation, the bad cop said to the other, "What are we going to do with him?"

The "good" cop said, "Let him go this time, but don't ever let us catch you speeding again!"

My next youthful encounter with police mischief occurred some months later. I worked part-time at the *Atlanta Constitution* newspaper, loading trucks overnight with bundles of daily newspapers and delivering them to drugstores, newsstands and other retail outlets.

By late Saturday afternoon, the early Sunday edition of the paper was published. This portion of our work was finished around 8 p.m., after which we repeated the same routine to deliver the "City Edition"—the later edition—of the newspaper. This part of the job lasted until approximately 4:30 Sunday morning.

There was, of course, no public transportation running at that time of morning. Consequently, on weekends, my dad permitted me to use the family car for going back and forth to work.

Finishing my shift, I headed out and waited for a red light to change at the corner of Spring and Peters streets. As I sat there, the motor idling, an Atlanta police car pulled up behind me, and purposely bumped my car.

I was faced with the no-win dilemma of what to do about it. Obviously, it would have made no sense to start a conversation with these white police officers considering their traditional bad attitude toward African-Americans.

For lack of any other solution, I got out of the car, walked around to the back of my car, looked at the bumper, and saw, with great relief, there was no damage done. (Not that there was anything I could have done about it even if there were any damage.) I got back in my car and drove away as they were busy laughing at this joke they had pulled on me. They seemed to have greatly enjoyed it, but I did not see the humor in it at all.

•••

My next encounter with the Jim Crow South was on the way home from school one day while I was a student at Booker T. Washington High. The school was downtown—a long trip every day to get to class and safely back home again.

I often caught the No. 19 streetcar on what was then Ivy Street, behind the Georgia Power building in downtown Atlanta.

I was in line to board the streetcar when a burly white man came out of nowhere to aggressively push me out of line.

"Boy," he said, "don't you know you are not supposed to stand in line in front of a white girl?"

I was deeply angered, offended and psychologically hurt. But I backed away from the streetcar without saying a word, lacking any legal recourse. No one came to my defense. Reporting the incident to the police would have been fruitless.

Instead, I walked away, blood boiling, and headed toward Decatur Street. I went into the first pawnshop I saw and spotted a .25 automatic, pearl-handled pistol for $15. I gave the man behind the counter $5 as a down payment to hold the gun. I was still working part-time at the newspaper and promised that as soon as I earned enough to pay the balance, I would be back.

Two weeks later, I was back in the store with the balance and enough for a box of ammunition.

The next white man who assaulted me—or offensively put his hands on me without cause—would die right then and there because I would kill him.

For the next few weeks, I carried the loaded pistol around in my pocket wherever I went. I told no one about it, and I felt confident for whatever came my way.

In a less guarded moment one Saturday, my dad and I were turtle gigging in Nickajack Creek. Turtle gigging involved walking along the creek in the shallow areas, sometimes on the bank, and running a "gig" under it to root out turtles.

We were startled by the appearance of a water moccasin—what many people might know better as a cottonmouth snake, a venomous pit viper.

In my excitement, I reached in my pocket and pulled out my .25, which I had practiced with and learned to shoot well, and shot the snake dead.

My dad, I'm sure, was in a state of shock that I matter-of-factly pulled a pistol out of my pants and started firing. To his eternal credit, he said nothing at the moment.

Later that day as we were in the car, en route home, Dad asked me why I felt the need to have this weapon. I told him what had happened at the streetcar and what I did in response.

He understood and sympathized with my position, but also soundly advised me that this was not the correct course, that I should not do myself the long-term harm of having to face the results of killing a man if it came to that. He wanted me positioned to effect change—for me and everyone else.

In his calm and wise fashion, he said that I was on the verge of letting one white man's hatred and untoward behavior ruin my life, which would give this man, if he lived to survive it, great pleasure. Dad talked to me in a level tone, showing me respect as a young man, not a boy, and nothing else was ever said about the matter.

I soon went back to focusing on my schoolwork and childhood and forgot about the weapon.

I think back on that day often. It is abundantly clear to me that God intervened in events by sending the snake into my path and saving my life. Had it not appeared where and when it did, there is no telling what eventually would have happened. Whatever, it would not have been good.

By the way, I never knew what happened to that pistol. Somewhere along the way it disappeared, and that was probably the best thing that could have happened to me.

9. COLLEGE: A RETURN TO TUSKEGEE

When I was a senior in high school, it was understood that I would be the first member of our family to attend college. I had no idea what I wanted to major in or what I wanted to do thereafter. The only thing I knew was that I wanted to pursue a career that would enable me to climb the economic ladder and to enjoy the kind of livelihood and respect we had known when we lived in Tuskegee.

I chose Tuskegee Institute because the community was a second home to me, having lived there quite happily and fruitfully as an adolescent. The city was a boomtown when we lived there. Going back there for college felt natural, even preordained.

My other options would have been the historic black colleges in Atlanta—Clark College, Morehouse College or Morris Brown. But Tuskegee was where I felt at home. And several of my friends, including Herman, felt the same way.

One day I saw a movie called "The Fountainhead." This 1949 film was written by Ayn Rand, directed by King Vidor, and starred Gary Cooper, Patricia Neal and Raymond Massey. It chronicled the fictional life of Howard Roark, a world-famous architect. I decided right away, after I saw the creativity that Roark (played by Cooper) put into his work, that designing buildings was the life for me.

Unfortunately, colleges in Georgia were still segregated at the time, and there was nowhere in Georgia that a black person could study architecture. Tuskegee Institute, in Alabama, did not offer architecture as a major, but it did offer a major in commercial industries with a minor in architecture. Having happily lived in Tuskegee as a child, I decided that this was where I wanted to attend college.

Tuition at the time was $300 per year, and room and board was $40 per month. Tuskegee Institute did not have much money for scholarships or student assistance and I was only able to obtain a small student loan.[7]

Soon after starting my freshman year, it became apparent that architecture was not for me. The glamor of "The Fountainhead" was elusive to say the least as my creative design skills were nonexistent. I couldn't draw a four-sided outhouse. In fact, the first project we were assigned in the architecture class was to design a gazebo. I didn't even know what a gazebo was! No idea. Remember that for about half of my life, I had lived in a situation where we did not have an inside toilet. The first house I designed in school did not have an inside toilet.

I did do well in the academic parts of the course, i.e., history of architecture and engineering. And I made a friend from Birmingham, Norva Harris, who was a talented designer but poor at the academic parts of the course. We made a great pair, as he helped me do my design work and I helped him with his academic exploits.

•••

Our dormitories at Tuskegee were World War II Army barracks, which left a lot to be desired. Two male students were assigned to each room, with a community shower and washroom at the end of the hall.

To supplement my finances, I started a business in my freshman year. I went to the boys' dormitory and picked up their clothing for laundry and dry cleaning. I took it to Reed's Dry Cleaning on Old Montgomery Highway, and after cleaning, I returned the clothes to the dorms. I retained 10 percent of all the monies I collected. I, of course, had no means of transportation at that point, so I did this work by carrying loads of clothes back and forth on my back.

While on campus, we had our meals at Tompkins Hall. The girls' dormitory, White Hall, was just across the park, a.k.a. "Lovers Lane."

If a boy wanted to have a date with one of the girls, we had to meet at their dorm and properly escort them for lunch, dinner, a movie or a sporting event, and return them safely—and before curfew—after the date. We

---

[7] Interesting side note: Because architecture was exclusively offered in white colleges that I could not attend in Georgia, I discovered by my sophomore year that there was a law requiring the state of Georgia to pay my tuition at Tuskegee. This change in the status quo dramatically improved my financial situation. I collected this subsidy for the last three years of my study at Tuskegee, but missed the first year because I knew nothing about the program, and nobody bothered to tell me about it.

had to say goodnight to our dates outside, as we were not allowed in the women's dormitory.

One night I was saying goodnight to my date, and Mrs. Hattie B. West, the dean of women, came out of nowhere, and chastised us for kissing on our way from the mess hall. (I knew Mrs. West all too well; she was previously the principal of the Chambliss Children's House Elementary School when I was a student there.)

"Mr. Ward, I am ashamed of you," she said.

Am I doing it wrong? I wondered to myself.

All I did was share a chaste, innocent goodnight kiss, but she dressed me down as if she caught me red-handed, trying to get to second base. Her position was that, instead of being a judge of the student court, I deserved to be brought on an Honor Code violation before the court.

She did not turn me in, but I felt as small as a mustard seed.

•••

After two years of dorm life, my Atlanta friends—Herman J. Russell, Jimmy Haynes, William Kimbrough and Raymond Dumas—plus Norva Harris (he was from Birmingham) and I—decided to move off campus.

We rented a three-bedroom house at 111 Church St., owned by the Reverend Kelly. Each of us kicked in the money we would have paid for lodging on campus, along with our mess hall allowance, to cover our rent and food bill, and even hired a cook to prepare our meals.

Kimbrough was reared by his grandmother and he had grandmotherly type ways. He was the stabilizing member of our group. He was the one who coached and steered us to always do the right thing. He was the mother hen in our group and a great friend to this day.

Tuskegee Institute had a big nursing program, and the John A. Andrew Memorial Hospital was on campus. That meant we got to know a lot of nurses and nursing students. I have nothing but warm memories about them because we had a good time with the nurses. They wore beautiful uniforms with maroon and blue capes. For us, a female in a nursing uniform was eminently more desirable than a woman in any other uniform.[8]

Somewhere along the way, Herman met Otelia Hackney—his future first wife—and she came down to visit us a few times at Tuskegee, so that kind of slowed Herman down some.

Alcohol was not a big thing. If we went to a nightclub, alcohol was not on the menu because none of us could afford it. And we didn't have

---

[8] Herman and I tried to coach Kimbrough—a bachelor—in later years, "Don't talk about 111 when we're all together with our wives!" Kimbrough didn't have a wife, so he never quite understood that our *wives* didn't want or need to hear about our college dating experiences.

alcohol at 111. We just didn't. Nobody wanted it, I guess.

We always had a good time at 111 Church St., but looking back, I regret that we did not spend more time on campus, participating in school activities. That said, I was still elected president of our sophomore class, and chief judge of the Student Court.

By our senior year, one or two of the guys dropped out, so we didn't need that big house anymore. Herman, Kimbrough, Norva and I rented a less expensive, two-bedroom place back on campus. It didn't have a shower in it, so we had to walk across the lawn to the basement of the landlord to use his shower. We did have a few parties there occasionally and had a great time.

•••

Male students at Tuskegee Institute were required to do two years of Junior ROTC.

I voluntarily chose to continue forward into the Senior ROTC. I did so for practical reasons; we were paid 90 cents a day. Many times, that was the difference between eating good, healthy food and not eating good, healthy food.

I was promoted to company commander of my ROTC unit, one of two on campus. In this role, it was my job to direct what is called a close activity drill formation, the practice of which we became highly proficient.

I thoroughly enjoyed the ROTC training. We were required to attend chapel services on Sundays, and the ROTC cadets and nurses marched to and from there, led by the Tuskegee Institute Marching Band. It was a delightful event, full of military pageantry and a great part of living in the city of Tuskegee. Persons from far and near would come out on Sunday mornings to watch the parade go by.

I had no thought of a military career at that point; it was just another way to survive. Even after I was eventually commissioned as a second lieutenant, a military career had not found its way into my plans for life.

At that point, if I went all the way through ROTC, I had an obligation to at least one three-year military term. I received a college deferment because, in July 1953, the war in Korea was winding down, and everybody who graduated from college with a commission otherwise expected to be called to active duty. But the Army didn't need all these people, so it stopped calling us to active duty. My deferment to finish college—fortunately—took me past the end of the war, so I missed the Korean War by a few months.

I don't recall being nervous about it—I don't think my parents ever discussed it with me, either—but a lot of young officers called up ahead of me were killed in Korea. We all thought that we were immortal, so from the comfort of Tuskegee, I didn't worry too much about being shot over there. But we were certainly conscious of the fact that the mortality rate was high.[9]

•••

One of my high school friends in Tuskegee was Bobby Larkin. Bobby grew up in Tuskegee, but went away to college. His mother and father still lived in Tuskegee. Once they found that I was back, they often invited me to their home for Sunday dinner. Considering that the cafeteria food on the campus left a lot to be desired, going to the Larkin family home was always a highlight of my week.

Mr. Larkin was a watchmaker. Back when my family lived in Tuskegee, my mother's youngest brother, David, came to visit us and he let me wear his wristwatch to school one day. We always played basketball during recess, and some rough play knocked the watch off my wrist and it came crashing to the ground. The crystal shattered and one of the hands broke.

Lucky me: I knew Mr. Larkin. I took it to him to be repaired, not knowing exactly how I would pay for his work. When I went to pick it up, Mr. Larkin said, "Felker, there is no charge."

•••

I always went to the post office hoping to get a letter from my mother, because she always included two dollars in it. There were times that money was so scarce for me that I would buy a candy bar, as opposed to something healthy to eat, because it would help satisfy my appetite.

While I was in college, my dad had a mild heart attack. Money became a real challenge for me as a student and my family back home, so I worked harder. There had been no time in my life since the age of 10 that I didn't have some kind of job.

A gentleman who was influential in my childhood, Mr. Charles Smallwood, had a paper route in the Tuskegee community. I rode with him to deliver papers when I was in elementary school. When I returned to town for college, Mr. Smallwood drove a taxi during the day and worked as a telephone operator at the Veterans Administration Hospital at night. We made a deal whereby I drove his taxi at night. This was difficult for me, but I needed the money. The taxi stand where we waited for outcalls was where I did my homework and studied between taxi runs. I made pretty good money, but needless to say, being up most of the night and at school

---

[9] As an adult, I later discovered a coincidental linkage to my time at Tuskegee and my ROTC service. We were issued Springfield M-1 rifles to use in our drills, and the person in charge of the storage room for the rifles—the armorer—was Mr. Henry Moore. It turns out that my future wife, Mary, was his niece!

during the day took its toll. That taxi was in use 24 hours a day.

As a result of those jobs, I missed out on what otherwise would have been a lot of fun on campus, I guess. But that's what I did. That's what I needed to do.

•••

One night, a friend and I were driving separate cars back to town from a juke joint on Highway 29 called "The Last Chance." Macon County, where Tuskegee Institute was located, was a dry county, so if we wanted beer, we had to go to the next county over, which was Bullock County, where "The Last Chance" was located.

On the way back, we were driving at a fairly good clip, not really racing, but an observer might have thought otherwise. Out of nowhere came Macon County Sheriff Preston Hornsby Sr. He drove a black Ford with an 8-foot whip radio antenna.

That antenna danced back and forth for what seemed like an eternity after he stopped us. Sheriff Hornsby ordered us to follow him back to the county jail, where he booked us for street racing. We could not leave until we either paid the fine—$35—or put up a bond, neither of which I had.

I called my dad, who caught the first bus to Tuskegee and bailed me out. We drove back to Atlanta together, and the first few miles of the drive was spent in utter silence.

Finally, dad broke the silence.

"I was glad Sheriff Hornsby said that, at least, y'all had not been drinking."

The truth is, we probably had had one or two (or three) beers, but we did not consume much alcohol at all, and we were certainly not intoxicated. I suspect that Sheriff Hornsby[10] knew that we had had a few beers, but chose not to lower the boom on us. I was relieved, but not surprised at my dad's reaction. He was a person who, under practically any and all circumstances, would find a way not to be accusatory, and to allow anyone an honorable way out of whatever the situation was.

•••

Because of the school promotions that I had received in elementary and high school, I completed college at the tender age of 20. In fact, I turned 20 the same month I graduated from Tuskegee Institute.

---

[10] Later in life, through my service on the Tuskegee University Board of Trustees, I became friendly with a fellow trustee named Alec Hornsby. We have, on occasion, hunted quail together. As it turned out, Alec was the son of Sheriff Hornsby. He laughed the first time I told him about my professional encounter with his father. He told me that Sheriff Hornsby hired the first black deputy sheriffs in the state of Alabama.

Tuskegee University

By authority of the Board of Trustees and upon recommendation of the faculty, Tuskegee University hereby confers upon

Felker William Ward, Jr.

the degree of

Bachelor of Science

in Commercial Industries

with all the rights, honors, and privileges appertaining thereto.

Given at Tuskegee, Alabama, this month of October, 1988

Chairman, Board of Trustees

President

Registrar

This Document Confirms the Degree Conferred by Tuskegee Institute, May 18, 1953.

This almost resulted in my undoing with respect to the military. I had already been deferred from active duty to finish college, and by the time I finished, the Korean War was over.

Then, even though I had taken all of my ROTC courses, and earned my eligibility to be a second lieutenant, I could not yet be commissioned in the Army because you had to be 21. This was a dilemma for me and for the Army. I had a choice of waiting a year before my commissioning and call to active duty, or going on active duty as an enlisted person for one year, and then receiving my commission.

Just before graduation day, my ROTC instructor investigated further and discovered that I could receive a reserve commission as a second lieutenant even at the age of 20. As a result, I was awarded a reserve commission on graduation day and was called to active duty as a second lieutenant. Subsequently, there was no time loss or setback for me.

•••

I thoroughly enjoyed my time as a student at Tuskegee. I did well in my studies at the Institute—making the Honor Roll each year—enough to rate an invitation to the National Honor Society.

I graduated on May 20, 1953, followed by my call to active military duty on September 30 of the same year.

•••

I live and breathe the spirit of "The Tuskegee Song."

In honor of Tuskegee University's 25th anniversary in 1906, Paul Laurence Dunbar was asked by the school's founder, Booker T. Washington, to write a poem capturing the Tuskegee spirit. This is what Dunbar wrote:

The Tuskegee Song[11]
by Paul Laurence Dunbar

I

Tuskegee, thou pride of the swift growing South
We pay thee our homage today
For the worth of thy teaching, the joy of thy care;
And the good we have known 'neath thy sway.
Oh, long-striving mother of diligent sons
And of daughters whose strength is their pride,
We will love thee forever and ever shall walk
Thro' the oncoming years at thy side.

---

[11] https://www.tuskegee.edu/student-life/join-a-student-organiza-tion/choir/the-tuskegee-song

II

Thy Hand we have held up the difficult steeps,
When painful and slow was the pace,
And onward and upward we've labored with thee
For the glory of God and our race.
The fields smile to greet us, the forests are glad,
The ring of the anvil and hoe
Have a music as thrilling and sweet as a harp
Which thou taught us to hear and to know.

III

Oh, mother Tuskegee, thou shinest today
As a gem in the fairest of lands;
Thou gavest the Heav'n-blessed power to see
The worth of our minds and our hands.
We thank thee, we bless thee, we pray for thee years
Imploring with grateful accord,
Full fruit for thy striving, time longer to strive,
Sweet love and true labor's reward.

•••

A few years after graduating from Tuskegee Institute, I received a letter from Mr. Charles Gomillion. Mr. Gomillion was the dean of men when I was a student, and also my English and literature teacher. He had seen a newspaper article with my name in it, and he wrote the letter to say, "If this is the same Felker Ward whom I taught as a student at Tuskegee, congratulations to you, and if not, please pardon my intrusion."

Mr. Gomillion had a tiny, squiggly handwriting style, and I recognized it immediately. I still have that letter.

One of the most important cases in the annals of constitutional law is the 1960 Supreme Court case of *Gomillion v. Lightfoot*[12]. The plaintiff in the case, Gomillion, was, indeed, the same Charles Gomillion who was my professor at Tuskegee.

Lightfoot was the mayor of Tuskegee, and Gomillion brought the case for the sake of outlawing the practice of gerrymandering real estate in the

---

[12] **Gomillion v. Lightfoot**, 364 U.S. 339 (1960). **Gomillion v. Lightfoot**. No. 32. Argued October 18-19, 1960. Decided November 14, 1960.

May 13, 1992

Dear Mr. Ward,

Thank you for your letter of recent date. It was good to hear from you. Some few years ago, a college mate, Bathell C. Wright, informed me that she had seen you and Mrs. Ward at a church, and that she had been in your home.

On the afternoon of March 31, I saw Margaret W. Clifford at The White House. On

54

2

the same afternoon, I saw Dr. B. F. Payton. I have not been to Tuskegee since June, 1988.

I think that 1993 will be the 40th anniversary of the class of 1953. I am selfish enough to wish that I could be on campus to see its members celebrate. Many of the members of the class are to be congratulated on their success in their various, and varied,

3

careers.

Dr. Robert T. Dibble, our family physician, has told my niece and me that "you two are about as well off as you could expect to be considering your ages." (Blondetia is 89 and I am 92.) Dr. Dibble saw us last on Easter Sunday afternoon.

Best wishes for con- tinued good health,

Sincerely,

C. G. Gomillion

city, for the purpose of thwarting the right and opportunity of African-Americans to vote. White politicians drew the city limits along a given street, and when they came to the home of an African-American, they went around that house and gerrymandered it out of the city. This practice became most prominent after it became apparent that voting rights were about to be federally protected, and this was an attempt on the part of white citizens to maintain political control of the city and the county.

It became one of the most important cases in the Civil Rights struggle of the 1950s and '60s.

II. ARMY DAYS,
BLUE SKY DREAMS

10. FIRST STOP: FORT BENNING, GEORGIA

The Korean War ended just before I graduated, and I never had any thought whatsoever of making a career of the military. Tuskegee was an industrial college; I studied commercial industries with a major in masonry, just like Herman, and thought I would serve my country for three years and pursue construction in civilian life.

At one point, Herman and I even entertained the idea of combining our skills after college and opening a construction enterprise.

But when I finished college in 1953, the job opportunities for a young African-American male with a college degree were few, other than teaching in the public school system. I had a military obligation to fulfill because of my ROTC service. The military was a good opportunity for a person in that time and of my makeup. It had a long way to go in terms of recognizing its role in society and what it needed to be about, but the military has always been one step ahead of the rest of the country.

•••

During the summer following my May 1953 graduation from Tuskegee Institute, I took a job at Lockheed Aircraft in Marietta, Georgia, to keep me busy and earn some money until my Army orders came through. Lockheed was building the C-130 Hercules military transport, and I started as a "structural assembler." That was a fancy name for a guy who was driving rivets or bucking rivets in the parts we were assembling. Since I had had training at Tuskegee in blueprint construction and reading, I applied that skill in assembling parts for the airplane.

We were on our feet all day, and it was fairly taxing. Several college friends of mine were also hired by Lockheed and we carpooled every day. I was happy to be living at home with my family, the pay was good, the work enjoyable and being with friends made the time fly by.

That was important to me, perhaps more than them, because I knew that, come Sept. 30, 1953, I belonged to the United States Army for the next three years.

•••

When the big day came, I reported to Fort Benning, Georgia, to begin my basic infantry officers training (BIOC).

BIOC was held in the Harmony Church area of the base. I had spent the summer between my junior and senior years in ROTC training in the Sand Hill area of Fort Benning, so I already knew my way around.

We received leadership training as well as combat arms warfare training in tactical subjects such as map reading, operational orders, survival training and the like.

More important than the subject matter, this was only my first brush with racial integration of any kind, other than the train ride to Connecticut. During my earlier ROTC training at Sand Hill, my unit was entirely composed of African-Americans.

My early experience in a racially integrated environment was uncomfortable. My prior experience with whites had always been unpleasant.

It didn't help that all of our leaders and commanders were white. It was clear that some of the white students were ill at ease working alongside black soldiers. We were as foreign to many of them as they were to us. In addition, civilian life in Columbus, Georgia, itself was substantially segregated. The whole circumstance was awkward, to say the least. When we were off-duty, we did not mix with our white counterparts. The few black officers like myself sought out black-owned restaurants, theaters and entertainment.

In the course of our daily activity, we frequently were bused from place to place for training. I noted that the white soldiers would not take a seat next to me. Consequently, I sat alone, mostly. There was no socialization with the blacks and whites in other units, either.

Another example of the lack of integration: I recall being told by a major, who was my boss, how to address my subordinates. No white officers received that instruction. I was frequently reminded that while integration was officially the order of the day, it was not welcomed nor embraced by many of my fellow soldiers and officers.

Eventually, this problem moved beyond socialization.

The military assignment system is one in which job titles and experience become important in later consideration for promotions. We did not have any senior African-American officers to help assist us in finding the appropriate assignments for moving up the ladder; we had few white sponsors available for advice and assistance. As a result, we found ourselves being cautious and careful about what we did, what we said and with whom we associated.

"Ticket-punching" is an important element of future military promotions. Ticket-punching means that there are certain jobs you need on the way up in the Army or any other industry. It means getting the correct assignments as you climb your way up the ladder.

We were organized in groups of 50 second lieutenants, with a first lieutenant officer in charge.

My officer was white, and I told him that I wanted to apply for flight school and asked him to help arrange for my application.

His response?

"In the first place," he said, "you're not going to get accepted into flight school. And number two, even if you are, you're not going to make it. You'll wash out."

In the moment, the racist message and intent behind what he said went right over my head.

"That might be true," I said. "But I want to apply anyway."

And I did. And he was wrong on both counts.

I was accepted, and I did not wash out. In fact, I excelled, having achieved the highest ranking in the class in both flight and ground school, but more about that later.

•••

Where the Army intended to send me was of less consequence to me than what it might train me to do: I wanted to be a pilot. That's what was driving me. My fascination for flying had its roots in my childhood at Tuskegee. I was thrilled to see the black cadets and pilots flying planes in and around Tuskegee. I thought, "Someday, I will do that, too."

The first time I went up in a plane was with Mr. Charles Smallwood in Tuskegee. Mr. Smallwood was a man I met when I was in elementary school. He had a newspaper delivery route and I subcontracted a part of that route from him. The next time I met him was when he was a flight instructor for the Tuskegee Airmen. It was a small, single-engine Cessna.

One day he said, "Have you ever been flying, Felker?"

I said no.

"You want to go?"

"Yes, sir!"

He had access to a plane at Moton Field and took me up for my first ride at dusk. I'll never forget it. We flew from Tuskegee over to Montgomery, which was about a 20-minute flight, and circled back.

By the time we returned, it was dark. There were no lights on the runway, and I wondered how in the world we were going to find it! As it turned out, there were automobile tires lined up on both sides of the runway, and the rubber was painted white so pilots could see them at night.

11. ON TO BERLIN

Upon completion of BIOC, my first active-duty assignment in January 1954 was in Germany. In the summer of 1954, I was reassigned to a battalion of the 6th Infantry Regiment in Berlin.

This was the first opportunity to put all of my training to good use, starting as a platoon leader in charge of 44 soldiers, which is the job of a second lieutenant. We spent a great deal of time on field maneuvers, rehearsing and exercising toward readiness for war.

•••

The regiment was headquartered in the Washington, D.C., area, but the battalion to which I was assigned was in Berlin, about a hundred miles inside of East Germany, which was controlled by the Soviet Union. As a result, it was completely surrounded by Soviet units, which were allied with East Germany.[13]

Berlin, of course, had been the capital of Germany until the end of World War II, and it was—until then—the most important city in the country. To say the least then, it was a most awkward situation to have the Soviet Union, which was one of the Allied powers during World War II, in control of this major city. Any vehicular traffic between Berlin and the rest of Germany (or Europe) had to traverse a hundred miles of Soviet-controlled East Germany. On any given day, without warning, the journey could turn deadly.

---

[13] Some of the information used in this section comes from my memory of events; I also relied in part upon "The Big Rape," a 1952 novel by *Esquire* magazine war correspondent James Wakefield Burke.

In February 1945, when it became clear that it was only a matter of time before the Axis powers—and the Nazis in particular—would fall, the Allied forces convened conferences in Yalta and Potsdam for the purpose of deciding how a conquered Germany would be occupied and governed following the war. Attending the Yalta conference were President Franklin Delano Roosevelt, British Prime Minister Sir Winston Churchill and Soviet Premier Joseph Stalin.

During these meetings, two major agreements were reached: 1) it was agreed which forces would be responsible for the conclusion of the war; and 2) it was decided how a vanquished Germany would be governed after the war.

World War II officially ended in Europe on May 8, 1945, but the celebration began with the unconditional surrender of the Nazi forces to Gen. Dwight Eisenhower in a schoolhouse the night before. By that point, the American forces had reached the Elbe River at Magdeburg, about 100 miles southwest of Berlin, with the British forces at Lauenburg (a.k.a. Lauenburg an der Elbe).

With respect to the first major agreement, British and American forces had advanced to the Elbe River, roughly 100 miles west of Berlin. The Soviets, at the time, had reached an area of the River Oder, which formed a commercial link between Poland and Berlin. For the two forces to meet face-to-face in Berlin would have created a dangerous situation. The resulting agreement, therefore, was that the American and British forces would remain at the Elbe River and permit the Soviet forces to overtake Berlin.

As it turned out, the Soviets not only took Berlin but also continued their march westward until meeting up with the British and American forces along the Elbe. This resulted in Berlin being a hundred miles inside Soviet-controlled Germany—a far different result than the Allies expected following the Yalta accords.

Of all the major decisions in World War II, this agreement represented the greatest Allied blunder of them all. Here were two major, powerful forces, the United States and Great Britain, sitting idly along the Elbe River, while the Soviet Union not only took Berlin, it also established a foothold in the city that would prove historically advantageous to the Soviet Union.

When it was time for the Soviets to permit British, French and American troops to enter Berlin, it refused to do so, and Soviet forces continued their "rape" of Berlin for some months thereafter. Not until this occupation was well along did the Soviet Union move to honor the agreement it had made regarding the occupation of Berlin.

A second agreement reached at Yalta called for Berlin to be divided into four sectors, with roughly one-half of the city to be occupied by the Soviet Union, and the other half to be shared by the British, French and Americans. The governance of Berlin was to be in the form of an inter-Allied authority called the Kommandatura (Alliierte Kommandantur in German), with each of the four powers represented. By the time the Kommandatura was put in place, however, the Soviets occupied key government offices, judicial and communications centers. It took control of Berlin's treasuries, including its banks, government buildings, libraries and other major institutions.

The only facility of great importance that was included in the U.S. sector was Berlin Tempelhof Airport. Prior to pulling out of that sector, the Soviet Union went to great lengths to destroy the facilities at Tempelhof. This act represented the beginning of the Cold War.

On June 24, 1948, the Soviet Union unilaterally decided to blockade and restrict vehicle traffic along the autobahn, the national highway developed by Adolf Hitler and connecting all of Germany. Publicly, the Soviets claimed that the road was under repair. In addition, they would not permit any rail or barge traffic to enter Berlin. The blockade lasted until May 12, 1949. During that time, the U.S. and its allies transported, by air, up to 8,000 tons of goods and supplies per day, and ultimately 2.3 million tons total. It was known as the Berlin Airlift.

On May 12, 1949, the Soviet Union accepted that the blockade had failed in its objective of preventing the creation of a West German nation-state, and it ended the blockade. Had the U.S. and its allies chosen to break through the blockade with force, war would have surely occurred.

•••

As military assignments go, Berlin was a great pleasure.

I was a first lieutenant, assigned as an executive officer of my battalion's C Company. My company commander was Capt. George Abbott, a veteran of World War II and Korea who proudly wore his combat infantry badge with star. He was an outstanding company commander and, most important, a teacher to those of us who were young officers assigned to him.

I learned a great deal about leadership and Army customs from Capt. Abbott. He taught me two things that I will always remember. He correctly recognized that I was too reliant on his impressions of my work and my attempts to make sure that he was always satisfied.

"Lt. Ward," he said to me, "it is not important that you worry about my opinion of you. It is more important that you worry about your subordinates' opinions of you or your performance. And it doesn't matter whether they love you or hate you, it is only important that they respect you, because if they respect you, they will follow your leadership and you will be successful as their leader. Thereby, I will have no choice but to rate you very highly."

The other lesson he taught me was this:

One morning, I was a few moments late arriving at work. I was expected to be on duty at 7:30 every morning. I probably had been out a little too late the night before and overslept.

Capt. Abbott said, "Never be late for duty, or for an appointment, for that matter. It is better, if you must, to report for duty on time, and then take a break, than to be late arriving."

He instilled in me the absolute importance of the reliability of on-time arrivals.

•••

Truth be told, my assignment in Berlin was something akin to being stationed in New York City. There was always plenty to do off-duty, and it was a very, very good assignment.

Our living quarters were well-appointed, with each unmarried officer having a one-bedroom apartment with a kitchen and living room in a complex located adjacent to Grunewald Forest. Grunewald is a large city park, akin to Central Park in New York City.

The 6th Infantry Regiment—including our battalion—was noted for its proficiency in drills and ceremonies. This aspect of our duty came easily to me because of my ROTC training at Tuskegee Institute.

During that time I was invited and encouraged by several other lieutenants—all white—to take up golf with them. I did so, and there was a period when we went to the golf course at some point almost every day. We took lessons every afternoon after work, and on Saturdays we played 36 holes, followed by 18 more on Sundays.

We formed a battalion golf team, and the battalion commander was enthusiastic about winning. As a result, we had every Wednesday afternoon off for practice, and we played against one of the other battalion teams every Thursday.

In most of the outfits of which I was ever a member, there have been few, if any, other black officers who played.

The military is hierarchical, so most of the people I played with were my age, approximately my same rank. That's just the way you associate with one another in the military. And they were all white. But we were comfortable with one another.

It was around that time that Gen. Eisenhower had a heart attack and, in typical all-or-nothing fashion, the Army responded by *requiring* that every officer have an afternoon off during the week for physical exercise. Our battalion easily met that requirement on the golf course.

Golf was something that I came to enjoy doing as much as hunting or bowling. Its objective was not to integrate; the goal was to go out and have a good time. Barriers were falling, slowly, as a result of our recreation choices.

•••

President Harry Truman issued Executive Order 9981 in 1948.

The effect and intent of the executive order was to direct the racial integration of America's military forces.

In 1953, Truman was succeeded by Eisenhower, and the order was still a work in progress. It was by no means fully enforced. Practically speaking, all of the senior officers across the Army were still white men. There were approximately nine African-American full colonels in the entire Army and just one general—Benjamin O. Davis Jr.

On paper, it was necessary that you be assigned to various command jobs commensurate with your rank to advance. African-Americans, however, were not assigned to command jobs commensurate with their ranks. While the executive order was technically in force, it was not reliably practiced.

During my stay in Berlin, there were several African-American officers among us who were Korean War veterans—and who held the rank of captain—yet not one of them commanded a company that called for the rank of captain.

•••

The University of Berlin offered German language courses on our military base. I studied and became fluent in German, which made life in the city much more enjoyable, especially the way it opened doors to associate with German families. The fact that I took the time to learn their language made a positive impression on them. Once they found out I could speak German, they spoke more naturally with me and made me feel far more welcome in their city and their homes.

Tensions were at their very worst between the United States and the Soviet Union, and many Germans told me, "You Americans took the wrong side in the war. If you'd sided with us (Germany), you would not have had this problem. So you're getting what you deserve from Russia."

Never mind all the Nazi talk about the purity of the white race, of course.

•••

Notwithstanding President Truman's 1948 military desegregation order, there was still racism emanating from the military in countless ways.

In Berlin, there were no African-American women on the U.S. bases for the growing number of African-American soldiers to date. Consequently, we dated German girls.

In Berlin, we had many official social functions—receptions and dinners for the unit. All officers were expected to participate. And everyone brought their wives or their dates, the vast majority of whom were local girls. I, like my counterparts, was dating a German girl, so I brought her to my first official social event at the base.

The next day, my captain called me into his office and said, "The commander contacted me and asked me to let you know that this is not acceptable. Dating white German girls is not acceptable."

Of course, there were no black German girls. In fact, there was only one black female in the whole command, and she was somebody's wife. Officers didn't have any choice. Either you dated a German girl, or you had nobody to date. The conditions were very unfavorable in that respect.

•••

One of the most interesting duties that I was assigned related to Spandau Prison in the British sector of West Berlin. The prison—operated by the Allies on a rotating basis—was where seven German high commanders convicted of war crimes during the Nuremberg Trials served their prison terms.

I was rotated through the prison with a unit of some 50 soldiers. By then, this gigantic, high-security prison was operating primarily to contain just one prisoner, Rudolph Hess, who could be seen walking daily around the inner wall of the prison wearing a heavy GI overcoat, even in the hottest of weather. (Spandau was demolished after Hess hanged himself there in 1987.)

12. TEXAS: LEARNING TO FLY

Wrapping up my duty in Berlin in December 1956, I then received my dream orders: attend flight school at Camp Gary, Texas, beginning in May 1957.

I drove my 1955 Mercury from Atlanta to El Paso, which is a long distance. It was even longer if you were a black man driving solo in 1956 across Jim Crow Alabama, Mississippi, Louisiana and Texas.

Was I concerned about my safety? Absolutely!

I took my six-shooter .32-20 revolver as well as a .270 Weathersby deer-hunting rifle that held three bullets and my 12-gauge Browning automatic shotgun—the plug removed so that it would hold five shells—and put them in the car within easy reach on the front seat.

If these SOBs attack me, I reasoned, *and if there's up to 14 of them, I'm going to kill all of them before I ever let them hang me. Until I run out of ammunition, I'll be shooting.*

That was absolutely the way I felt. I feared for my life in that situation.

Crossing into Mississippi, I pulled into a service station. An elderly white gentleman came out to pump gas for me.

"May I help you, sir? How much would you like, sir?"

I was floored. He was the complete opposite of what I expected. The kindness and respect in his tone blew me away.

Not all white folks are bad, I thought, *and not all black folks are good.* By that point in my life, I had traveled a bit on my own and with the Army, meeting people all over the world. When they heard about things that were happening in the South and in the East and in the big cities, they thought nothing but the worst of Americans. They thought it was an absolute lawless jungle. Many told me they would not dare come to this part

Felker Ward Jr., flight school graduate.

of the country to live.

I didn't know how it was going to work out, but I went as well-prepared as I knew how to be. I was not going to give up my life without a fight.[14] They might beat me, but some of them would be lying alongside

---

[14] If you think I was over-the-top in my preparations for driving alone across the Southern part of our country to Fort Bliss, Texas, in 1957,

me. That was my attitude.[15]

•••

There was a delay of several months before I could begin flight school so I was assigned as interim operations officer for a basic training.

El Paso was a city that grew on me over time, as I met people and learned my way around. Today there are brochures and civic groups in most military towns designed to welcome soldiers and help them feel

---

remember that I was only a few years removed from being attacked by a white man because I committed the offense of standing in line for a street-car ahead of a white female. If you think about conditions then—and now—you might better understand my fear. Police services that are supposed to be designed to protect *all* citizens have not done so even to this day. Consider these six high-profile events just before and since then, in which justice was repeatedly denied to African-Americans based on the color of their skin: 1) a Charleston, South Carolina, police officer shot an unarmed black man named Walter Scott in the back. A jury of 11 whites and one African-American found the officer was justified and would not find the officer accountable for this summarized execution; 2) a grand jury in Cleveland declined to indict a police officer who shot 12-year old Tamar Rice dead for holding a toy gun; 3) a Staten Island grand jury declined to indict the white officer who choked Eric Garner to death despite the presence of a video showing the victim did not resist arrest; 4) a jury in Sanford, Florida, could not find a basis for a guilty verdict against a "neighborhood watchman" who stalked and killed 17-year old Trayvon Martin; 5) a jury in Sumner, Mississippi, acquitted two white men who murdered 14-year old Emmett Till on August 28, 1955, beating him so severely that it was said that even his mother had a hard time recognizing him when his body was found; and 6) a jury in Ventura County, California, acquitted all four police officers who mercilessly beat Rodney King.

[15] Two years later, after I married, my wife and I had a similarly chilling experience driving cross-country along the same route, this time to Fort Wolters near Fort Worth, Texas. Gas station toilets were still segregated, but a few large corporate gas companies had broken down the system. We evaluated each station before we purchased gas. I would pull up, ask for a fill-up and, in the same breath, ask for a restroom key. If the attendant (these were the days of full-service pumps) stated that the toilet was not locked, I knew what that meant. I would cancel the fuel order and proceed to the next service station to purchase my gas. We almost ran out of gas a few times before we found an integrated gas station.

welcome. Back then, we were pretty much on our own—especially African-Americans in the South.

When it was time to leave five months later, I knew I would always have a place in my heart for the well-named Fort Bliss.

•••

When I finally reported to Camp Gary, Texas, for flight school in May 1957, I was one of approximately 100 cadets—including eight African-Americans—assigned to class 57-15.

I thoroughly enjoyed flight school. We were trained in various subjects, including theory of flight, aircraft maintenance, weather, navigation and emergency procedures. Our training was in the Cessna L-19/O-1 Bird Dog aircraft. (They were later used heavily in Vietnam.)

My first hurdle was to become proficient enough for the instructor to allow me to solo. I took to the controls easily and soloed after just eight hours of training, an average time for those who moved forward.

The L-19 was a neat, high-wing, single-engine airplane, one with a forgiving nature. It was ideal as a basic flight training instrument.

We had several "check" rides by instructors who, we were all convinced, had one mission in life and one mission only: to wash us all out. There was, naturally, great apprehension among the cadets, black and white, surrounding the check ride system. The first check ride was the worst. In fact, after their first check ride, a good number of cadets did wash out, including *all* seven African-American students not named Felker Ward Jr. The second check ride claimed a few more. I stood out more than ever before, in every training session, in every barracks, but I kept my head high, my eyes and ears open, and focused on the end goal.

We never knew when the instructors would think we were ready. We went out for our flight every day, and one day an instructor told you to pull over to the ramp on the side.

Then he got out.

"Give me three takeoffs and three landings. On your own."

All of a sudden I found myself all alone in the wild blue yonder. Relatively quiet. Nobody bothering me, nobody disturbing me, nobody verbally beating up on me. It was exhilarating to know that I made it, that I could truly fly like a bird. It was a feeling that you only got once. It was thrilling.

Subsequent check rides were not nearly as stressful. By then, it was apparent who would graduate—and who would not.

It's worth noting that the check ride was not with your instructor. It would be with some pilot whose whole job was to check a cadet's progress and make sure that he was going to succeed as a pilot.

I don't know what, exactly, caused those other seven black cadets to wash out. One day they were there, and the next day they were gone. So you don't really know what happened. I only know that I had a fair shot, notwithstanding any racial issues.

One of the things that got a lot of cadets in trouble was what's called a "ground loop." It was easy to lose directional control over the plane if you weren't careful. If that happened to you, it would almost guarantee you'd be put out of the program. Everybody feared that moment. And there were some check ride pilots who were worse than others. They were really, really tough on us. But I didn't have any problems.

Depth perception kept a lot of people from ever getting into the program. It's a defect in your vision that is fatal to flying an airplane.

After getting past the hurdle of soloing and the initial examination, I found flight school enjoyable and not anywhere near as taxing. Every day, we spent half of our time flying and half in the classroom, dealing with the various subjects we had to master.

The first four months were at Camp Gary, Texas; the next four were at Fort Rucker, Alabama. That's where we were introduced to more technical challenges. They taught us maneuvers with airplanes to support ground operations. We learned how to manage the airplane in unfavorable terrain. When I was done, I felt that I could do anything that airplane was designed to do.

At Fort Rucker, we were taught tactical techniques, operating on unimproved, short airstrips, cross-county navigation and advanced weather training.

I don't know how they selected who would teach whom, but somehow or other, I wound up with a good instructor, one who was very fair. He saw past the color of my skin; not all of them could. I only got one pink slip in the whole program. It was in the precision flying phase at Fort Rucker. I had already earned my wings and had entered the third phase of training, mainly instrument school, in which we were taught to fly under adverse weather conditions, including low visibility. They taught us to fly using only the instruments. In this program, 100 feet off altitude was enough to get me a pink slip. I daresay no one went all the way through flight school without getting at least one pink slip.

I got that one pink slip. The instructor was reluctant to give it to me because, normally, when you came off a flight where you've earned a pink slip, you'd get it right then. I got mine the next day.

"I decided I should have given you a pink slip yesterday," he said.

HEADQUARTERS
UNITED STATES ARMY AVIATION SCHOOL
Office of the Registrar
Fort Rucker, Alabama

SUBJECT: Class Standing

Date: 14 Dec 57

TO: Ward, Felker W.

    1. It is the desire of the Commandant, as well as the faculty officers, that each student be continuously cognizant of his progress while at the United States Army Aviation School.

    2. As of 14 December 195 7, your standing relative to that of the rest of your class is number 1 in a class of 68 students.

    3. Grade averages.

        Flight: 85

        Academic: 90.180

        Overall: 87.590

TAAC(TAAS) FL 30
7 May 57

JOHN O. GILLILAND
1st Lt   TC
Registrar

UNITED STATES ARMY AVIATION SCHOOL
OFFICE OF THE COMMANDANT
FORT RUCKER, ALABAMA

AASSC 201.22   14 December 1957

SUBJECT: Letter of Commendation

TO: First Lieutenant Felker W. Ward
        Army Aviation Tactics Course Phase B, Class Nr 57-15
        United States Army Aviation School
        Fort Rucker, Alabama

1. It is my pleasure to commend you for the splendid record you have established as honor student in the Army Aviation Tactics Course Phase B, Class Number 57-15, in residence during the period 19 September 1957 - 14 December 1957.

2. Your standing as number one in a class of 68 students reflects both your application to academic work and the degree of proficiency which you have attained in the techniques of flight.

3. The training you have received in this program is the best of its type in the world. Continuous application of the principles you have learned will enable you to contribute materially to Army Aviation and to perform further duty of great value to the military service.

BOGARDUS S. CAIRNS
Brigadier General, USA
Commandant

Navigation instruments were not plentiful in the Army at that time and we spent a great deal of time in a flight simulator. For cross-country navigation, one of our primary tools was the low-frequency radio navigation system. It was not especially reliable, and inclement weather had an adverse effect on our ability to navigate using that system. Nonetheless, we all mastered it and, after finishing flight school, I made quite a few instrument flights utilizing that system, as imperfect as it was.

There was one African-American student in the class ahead of me, 57-14; there were no others in my class besides me, 57-15. We got together some weekends when we were off and made friends. But it was not an environment in which you could strike up many other friendships. We had long workdays and, being in the South, there was abject discrimination. If you didn't have any other blacks there in the class with you, there was nobody to be friends with because we didn't go to the same restaurants, we didn't go to the same clubs, we didn't do anything together. More often than not, I was on my own.

There was a carry-over of the white soldiers' background and heritage into their military lives. A distinct demarcation line was drawn. Flight school was not all work and no play, but there was no integrated play. We did not hang out together.

I usually found myself to be the only African-American military man around. Or if not the only one, maybe one of two. Everyone, I guess, brought to their assignment, and our time together, their background from wherever they started, the way things were at home. There's a saying that the military is a microcosm of society. Well, I didn't have any white friends at home, either. I don't recall going to a single dinner with a white person while I was in flight school.

I'd go into town and get a meal occasionally by myself. One thing I always found good for me was that I knew the tricks. I almost always wore a uniform off base; that got me a lot of dates. I met a girl in a little restaurant one night. I was there alone, having dinner in civilian clothes. She came in alone, too, so I introduced myself to her. We got to know each other and eventually started dating. I dated her exclusively the rest of the time I was there. Her name was Rosa.

I got to know Rosa and her mother. I don't remember meeting her dad, though. Rosa was single, a widow whose husband had died tragically and left her to raise several children on her own. She had a couple of married sisters, so I got to know her extended family and spent time with them. But when I left Camp Gary, the relationship ended.

•••

At the end of training, we graduated and received our wings. My mother and father came from Atlanta for the ceremony, which delighted

My graduation photo from Fort Rucker, Alabama; I was first in my class. White shirts are instructors; students are in flight jackets.

me. This was my greatest accomplishment to date.

It was common practice at that time to call the roll of officers in alphabetical order to come forward for their wings. However, it was also practice that the honor graduate in the class was called first. As such, I was called first to receive my wings.

After the ceremony, many of the white parents in the audience congratulated my parents on my achievement.

"That must be your son," they heard over and over.

13. BACK TO FORT BENNING: MARY ENTERS MY LIFE

After graduating flight school in 1957, I was assigned to a flight detachment at Fort Benning's Lawson Field in Georgia.

Our group flew missions in support of the infantry school and a ranger training program in Dahlonega, Georgia. We rotated pilots through the program every week, operating out of a small airstrip in a cow pasture. The crew chiefs back at Fort Benning were always unhappy with the condition of the airplanes after returning from operations in a cow pasture for a week at a time.

One of the things we learned about supporting the rangers was that, inasmuch as we were in the skies above the north Georgia mountains, flying could be hazardous. There were extremely strong air currents, sometimes downdrafts, and we had to exercise more than common caution to avoid crashing. Also, if we were flying over a wooded area in north Georgia and saw smoke emanating from the woods, we were well-advised to stay clear of that area. In all probability, it was a moonshine operation, and they did not take kindly to planes interfering with their operation. Their rifles were known navigational hazards.

In addition to my flight duties at Fort Benning, I was assigned a staff job as deputy logistics officer for the base.

In that position, my immediate superior was Capt. Ben Fowler. Working with him provided me a valuable opportunity to learn the military logistics system, which proved valuable later when I was in Vietnam.

•••

The Officers Club at Lawson Field was frequented by pilots and paratroopers.

One night, we had all been imbibing a great deal. The pilots took a head count and discovered that there were as many of us there as there were paratroopers.

One of the pilots yelled across the room to another, "What do you think of a fellow who would jump out of a perfectly good running airplane, when he could land it and step out?"

Needless to say, that did not go over very well: A brawl followed. The next day, we were all called on the carpet and told that we had to pay to replace all the chairs and tables that had been damaged in the maelstrom of the previous evening.

•••

Eugene Cummings, a friend who followed me at Tuskegee and to flight school, caught up to me at Fort Benning and I was glad to see him.

We went on a blind double date one hot summer night. One of the young ladies was a nurse I already knew, but the other girl—whose sister orchestrated the blind date—was new to me. It was not long before it became apparent that the new girl, Mary E. Jamerson, was more attractive to me than the girl I already knew, and she apparently felt the same way.

Mary was beautiful. We honored the blind date for the evening, but from that night forward, Mary and I have been together.

We had a wonderful summer together.

Mary was home in Columbus for summer vacation between her junior and senior years at Clark College in Atlanta. We saw each other often during the remainder of the summer, and I was able, on occasion, to rent an airplane from the flying club at Fort Benning and take Mary for rides. In fact, the way I won her over for good was when I took Mary for her first airplane ride at Fort Benning.

"We met between my junior and senior years of college," Mary recalled. "My mom, Leanna, was a stay-at-home mother, because she had six children, five girls and one boy. Folks used to call my daddy 'The Hawk' because he sat up at night till all the chickens got in. My daddy would never go to sleep with anybody being out. Daddy worked with Central Georgia Railroad for 44 years. Back in the day, there was not much a black man could do; he worked in the rail yard and he worked there forever.

"My dad did not like for us to date soldiers. He said they were not reliable.

"But I went to an air show with my family, and Felker was flying in it. When the show was over, I met him by accident; one of my sisters, who was a nurse, knew him. I don't really recall him making a great impression on me that day.

"My sister was going to hook me up with a friend of hers, because Felker already had a girlfriend. The four of us went out and we got to talking. Later, he invited me out, alone. We probably went out to dinner. He says I was always hungry!

"A week later, we started dating steady.

"Six months later, we were married. We didn't waste a whole lot of time with dating.

"His mom wanted him to get married. That was a good thing, in my favor, because she thought he was getting too old to be single. He was 26.

"He was stationed at Fort Benning and he had orders to go to Korea next. He wanted to get engaged and marry when he returned from Korea. That's what *he* wanted to do. I told him no, we couldn't get engaged. We had to get married because I figured that if I let him go on to Korea, he'd find him another girlfriend!"

Besides being beautiful, Mary was smart, too—she got in good with my mother. Why did that matter? Because I was 26, a single, modestly good-looking commissioned officer and pilot in the Army Air Corps. I was happy in the status quo, not thinking about getting married. *No, sir!*

As far as I was concerned, everything in my life was already going real great. But Mary and my mother decided they wanted to change things. Back in those days, if you reached 26 years old and you weren't married, something was wrong. But it was not unusual for a soldier to date someone in one city, then move on to their next base and the next girl.

My "mistake" was meeting someone back at home where I was anchored and had roots! I often jokingly say they double-teamed me!

After six months of dating, "we"—the three of us, that is, Mary, my mother and I—decided to get married.

I went to Mary's father, Mr. John Cook Jamerson, to make my proposal official and proper. Fortunately, I was in good stead with him because I had become a Mason—just like Mr. Jamerson. He made it clear that since Mary and I were engaged, he would not accept any other boys showing up at his door to take Mary on a date. It was just fine with me!

My rapidly evolving life plan was that Mary and I would become engaged before my upcoming 13-month assignment in Korea and married upon my return.

Mary had other ideas.

Her counter-proposal was that we get married before I left for Korea. If we were married, she could live with my parents in Atlanta and complete her senior year at Clark under their roof. My mother loved Mary and they had quickly become fast friends. As a result, my mother told me that Mary's plan was superior to mine!

On Feb. 7, 1959, we were married by my father, the Rev. Felker Ward Sr., on the lawn of Mary's parents' home in Columbus. My college roommate Herman J. Russell was my best man; Mary's friend, Ann, was her maid of honor.

"Shortly thereafter," Mary said, "Felker went to Korea. I stayed that year with his parents and finished my school year at Clark. It worked out really well for me.

"Felker's mom was glad to have me, because she didn't have any girls, just three boys. She was glad to have a partner! She and I got along well. She was not a person who drove cars and stuff like that, so I could drive her around on Saturdays when we went shopping, and we'd get in trouble because we'd stay out all day with no dinner prepared for the men. We really enjoyed being together.

"Felker and I survived by writing letters to each other every day. Sometimes he couldn't, but most days he did. It was hard, but we managed.

"Living in the Ward household without Felker required a lot of adjustments on my part, and his parents' part, because they had to get used to, number one, having a girl in the house for the first time. And number two, they were religious folks. My family was religious, but not as religious as his people. There was a lot of give and take on both sides. But we worked it out."

14. MARRIED AND ALONE, PART 1:
WELCOME TO SOUTH KOREA, SOLDIER

Before heading to South Korea, I was assigned to helicopter training at Fort Wolters in Mineral Wells, Texas.

I had purchased an almost-new 1957 Cadillac, and Mary and I put everything we owned in that car to drive halfway across the country.

Upon arrival at Fort Wolters, we discovered that no provisions had been made for spouses and we, along with several other couples who arrived at the same time, were billeted in a building that had previously been a BOQ, which stands for bachelor officer quarters.

My latest round of training was in the Hiller H-23 helicopter. The course lasted three months. It was intense at the outset, but after we progressed, it became enjoyable. It was not unusual for us to chase varmints around in the desert with the helicopter until they would finally give up and climb into a hole of some sort.

I was, by this time, a first lieutenant, and my base pay and allowance had risen to $300 per month. Mary fed us for $30 per week, allowing us to save almost half of my salary each month.

Once we finally settled in decent quarters at Fort Wolters, we thoroughly enjoyed our time there as honeymooners. The Army had a recreation camp with trailers and boats for rental on Possum Kingdom Lake, a few miles west of Fort Wolters, and we availed ourselves of the recreation center on many weekends. When we weren't enjoying the great outdoors—Mary shared my love of fishing—we went shopping in nearby Fort Worth.

•••

Upon completion of helicopter school, I was assigned to the 7th Infantry Division at Camp Casey in South Korea.

Camp Casey was not far from the demilitarized zone (DMZ) that served as the boundary between North Korea and South Korea.

On a daily basis, an observation flight was conducted along the DMZ from one end to the other. It was important that a precise route be flown (close enough to the DMZ to observe if anything was going on; we were under strict orders to never accidentally cross into the DMZ). It was a four-hour round-trip flight, and it was extremely dull. Frankly, it was the most undesirable mission we had, but one which was fraught with danger if you accidentally crossed the border to North Korea.

Other than that, flying in Korea was interesting. We had few navigational aids; we had to memorize routes to the various places where we flew. On any given day, it was not unusual to fly three different missions with three different airplanes. The first might be at the controls of a Cessna L-19/O-1 Bird Dog, second, a de Havilland DHC-2 Beaver, and the third, a Bell UH-1 Iroquois helicopter.

Living conditions in our unit were fair. We lived in huts heated by oil-burning stoves. We had makeshift showers supported by 55-gallon drums that were filled with fresh water daily and warmed by fires built underneath. There were occasional movie nights, but for the most part we played a lot of volleyball during the day and poker in the Officers Club at night.

Life in South Korea could be somewhat boring. As a result, I took this opportunity to purchase a kit to build a stereo system and, over a period of several months, frequently working late into the night, I built an amplifier, record player and speakers. I will always remember the joy of finally plugging it in when it was completed and finding that everything worked according to plan. Of course, it was simply a matter of following the step-by-step instructions that came with the kit. The only new requirement was that you learned to solder wires together.

The military police, quartermaster detachment and flight detachment were all housed in the same compound. The quartermaster was the division's supplier of foodstuffs, clothing and other necessities. We had an excellent relationship among the three units; we provided transportation to the men any time they wanted to go to Seoul or anywhere else. The quartermaster, in turn, ensured that we always had the best available food rations. And the military police made sure we had few security issues.

There was a problem one night when a Korean man, who weighed a little more than 125 pounds, soaking wet, was caught leaving our compound with a 55-gallon drum of oil on his A-frame carrier. He made a desperate attempt to escape—and was unsuccessful.

I occasionally visited Seoul for weekend rest and recuperation (R&R)

to catch a good movie, eat at a fine restaurant and perhaps visit a nightclub. Having become a Mason, I enjoyed attending meetings at the Seoul Masonic Lodge once a month. I also could travel to Tokyo, Japan, where I was able to shop for items that were not readily available to soldiers in Korea.

From left: C.A. Scott, Brigadier General Daniel "Chappie" James, Mary Ward, Felker Ward Jr. James later retired as a four-star Air Force general.

15. FORT MEADE: HAPPY WIFE, HAPPY LIFE

Upon my return from South Korea, 13 months later, I was back at Fort Benning for an advanced officers' course.

On the personal side, I began my life as a true married man. Mary's sisters and their husbands lived in Columbus, and we were frequently together for family outings on the weekends. As a man who always enjoyed being with family, adding sisters- and brothers-in-law to the mix was a great deal of fun.

My time back home at Fort Benning was short-lived as I received a more permanent assignment to Fort Meade, Maryland. We packed our belongings and set out on the 10-hour drive from Columbus to Fort Meade.

After driving 10 hours north, Mary and I arrived at Fort Meade. But it was after 6 p.m. and once again there had been no provisions made for temporary quarters for us. I drove into downtown Baltimore and discovered that the city's hotels were still segregated. This was the North? How far north did a black person have to drive in 1960 to be treated equally? We were forced by circumstances beyond our control to spend the night in our car. Fortunately, we knew one family that lived in Baltimore and they accommodated us for several days. Thereafter, we rented a furnished apartment on Reisterstown Road, near the Mondawmin Mall in Baltimore. It took three months to rise on an officers housing waiting list and into family quarters.

What we encountered—and it was not unique to us—was that the Army's attitude in those days was that if it had intended for a soldier to have a spouse, it would have issued him one. Clearly, the Army of that era did a poor job of making provisions for families.

As an Army lieutenant, I was making approximately $300 a month, plus an extra allowance of $40 for food and clothing. But that was not a lot of money in Greater Baltimore.

Mary, who had earned a bachelor's degree in business administration from Clark College, with a minor in education, was always able to get a job no matter where I was assigned because good clerical help was in high demand.

My new wife did a wonderful job of taking a little bit of money and preparing all sorts of wonderful meals, so we never felt poor. She grew up in a family that didn't have a lot, and her mother—and mine—taught her how to stretch a dollar when it came to dinnertime.

•••

There is a saying that, "Flying an airplane is hours and hours of sheer boredom interrupted occasionally by moments of stark terror." I found this to be true.

One of those moments came when I was returning from a mission to Fort Knox, Kentucky. I had flown Maj. Gen. Raymond Bell, deputy commander of the 2nd Army, to Fort Knox, and when his business there was complete, we began the return trip to Fort Meade Airfield. There was a great deal of sleet and snow falling at the time, and our departure runway was covered in slush. The flight back was otherwise uneventful despite the weather … except when we arrived and I put the lever down to lower the landing gear and the two main wheels showed "Safe," but the nose wheel did not.

I was fairly confident that the nose wheel was down and locked in place, but I needed to be sure. I contacted the control tower at Fort Meade and asked them to have a pilot run up to the control tower, examine the plane as I flew by and give me his opinion.

A few moments later, the control tower radioed back and said, "Sir, all of the pilots are at the Officers Club for Happy Hour. They said, bring it in low and slow over the club, and they will let us know if the gear was down or not."

That was not a good solution!

Fortunately, in the course of this communication, I had been flying in above-freezing temperatures for 20 minutes when suddenly the nose wheel showed "down and locked." We landed safely.

Upon investigation, we later discovered that, in my takeoff from Fort Knox, the switch, which would signal a down and locked position for the nose wheel was frozen with ice in the "up" position. It was only after I had circled for 30 minutes in the lower altitude—and warmer temperature—that the ice on the switch melted and we got a safe indication. After I landed, I joined the rest of the pilots at the Officers Club, and I did not once have to buy drinks that night.

•••

My flight detachment at Fort Meade was commanded by Maj. Roy Buckwalter, and we flew Cessna L-19s, L-20s and the Beechcraft Twin Bonanza L-23 Seminole for 1st Army senior commanders and staff. The flights frequently took us to New York; Fort Knox, Kentucky; and Fort Belvoir and Fort Eustis in Virginia.

After my first year at Fort Meade, I was made a flight instructor for the Army area, which was comprised of most of the military bases in the Eastern Seaboard and west as far as Fort Knox and Fort Campbell, Kentucky.

In addition to flying the Beaver, I transitioned into twin-engine aircraft. Specifically, we flew the Beechcraft Model 50 Twin Bonanza, and subsequently received a Beechcraft Queen Air, which was the forerunner to the King Air. They both were fun to fly and, after a year in that assignment, I became the flight instructor for the 2nd Army. It was my duty to transition pilots who needed training from single- to multi-engine airplanes. This was perhaps the most fun assignment I ever had, and one that lasted for three years.

While stationed at Fort Meade, Mary was hired by the headquarters of the Army Corps of Engineers. Between her salary and my flight pay, we could afford plenty of recreational activities, and fishing in the Chesapeake Bay was one of the many highlights of our time at Fort Meade.

•••

Fort Meade also turned out to be an excellent assignment for us as a young couple still in the honeymoon stage of life.

Mary and I enjoyed fishing together, and we purchased a 17-foot boat with a 35-horsepower Mercury engine. We kept it on a trailer in the parking lot of our quarters, always ready for action out on the bay.

On one occasion, we had a harrowing experience when a sudden storm blew in, creating 3- and 4-foot waves. I maneuvered the boat close to the shore, so that in the event it capsized, we had a chance to survive.

Soon thereafter, we bought a 24-foot cabin cruiser with sleeping accommodations as well as a galley and head. I bought the boat in Baltimore and ferried it to Annapolis, where the boat was to be moored. By the time we reached Annapolis, it was nightfall, and I was not adequately familiar with the passage into the harbor. I navigated too close to the shore, hitting an underwater rock that knocked a hole in the hull of my new boat. I moved the boat off the rock and, with the help of a rag stuffed in the hole, along with the automatic bilge pump, safely made it to my dock. Lesson? Never go into an area at night with which you are not familiar.

This boat was moored at a dock owned by the Seafarers Yacht Club of Annapolis, which Mary and I joined.

We became close friends with three other couples at Fort Meade also assigned to the flight attachment: Lowell and Eunice Farris; Paul and Joyce Karas; and Pat and Janet Patterson. All three of these couples had young children, while Mary and I did not. A weekend rarely passed when our families were not together. Lowell was a chief warrant officer; Paul and Pat were both captains.

Annapolis was a 30-minute drive from Fort Meade, and we spent most of our summer weekends on the boat. It was close enough to base that even when I was on standby for any emergency pilot requirements, we could still get out on the water.

16. EUROPE CALLS ... AND I REFUSE A JOB

In 1963, after having been promoted to captain, it was the policy of the Army to require combat arms officers—of which I was one—but who were also pilots, to serve at least one year of "ground duty" in our basic branch—the infantry, in my case.

As company commander, I, along with the first sergeant, was responsible for complete equipment, training, promotions and overall general welfare of 156 men (there were no women in the ranks in those days). It was an extremely exhilarating job.

In the S-3 position, I was responsible for planning and execution of operations for a battalion consisting of five companies and approximately 800 soldiers. We were a mechanized infantry battalion and, as such, were extremely mobile.

I was assigned ground duty in Aschaffenburg, Germany, following my three years at Fort Meade. By this time, I was a senior captain and pretty close to being considered for promotion to major. It was important, therefore, that I solidified my captain command experience and senior staff position during the ground duty tour.

When I reported to Aschaffenburg, the new battalion commander—a lieutenant colonel who would have been my immediate boss—had not yet reported. Consequently, I instead reported to the brigade commander, a full colonel from Mississippi.

I stood in front of his desk, saluted, and said that I was "Capt. Ward, reporting for duty."

"Welcome, Capt. Ward," the colonel responded eagerly. "We are glad to have you, and have assigned you to be the battalion motor officer."

That surprised me—and not in a good way.

Being named the battalion motor officer was the most undesirable and unreliable assignment one could possibly have. It would not have been at all to my benefit as a rising major to have that assignment. It was typically given to officers and soldiers who were considered incapable of anything else, with nowhere to go in the military hierarchy. In other words, it was a dead end.

The motor pool was the place the brass often sent black officers and enlisted soldiers. The worst assignment you could draw was the motor pool.

I took a deep breath, slowly exhaled, and promptly put my career on the line.

A feeling rose within me that what I had to say was more important than what it might have meant to my career.

Still standing, I addressed this colonel and said, point-blank, to him, "I will not accept the battalion motor officer assignment.

"That," I continued, "is a job for a young lieutenant as an additional part-time duty, and if that is the only assignment you have for me in this brigade, I respectfully request an immediate reassignment."

The colonel rose from his seat, turned as red as a country beet, and yelled at me.

"What do you mean you refuse the assignment?!?"

He thought he was putting me in my place, but I was not intimidated by his rank or his race.

"I mean just what I said ... sir!"

He said, "How dare you tell me what you're not going to do."

"I just did, *sir*," I said.

And I meant it.

"I'm not going to be the motor pool officer."

This was not a good situation. I was an American military officer beholden to a system that did not always support men of my skin color. I literally knew no one in Aschaffenburg, no one who could attest to my qualifications, work ethic or anything else.

For the third time in my life that I know of, God intervened in a very, very forceful way.

It just so happened that the battalion commander, Lt. Col. Charles Clark, who was the command level between me and this colonel, was reporting in at the same time and was in the colonel's outer office. He heard the back and forth between us. Thank goodness, the door was wide open!

He hadn't been invited in, but he was within his rights. The way things work in the military, officers don't usually walk into rooms where they have not first been invited.

When Ltc. Clark came in—*another* white senior officer—I thought, "Oh, crap. Now there's two of them. I'm screwed."

And then the opposite happened.

Lt. Col. Clark entered the room, saluted, and told the colonel, "Capt. Ward will not be the motor officer. I am the battalion commander. I have looked over his 201 (experience file), and have already assigned him to a duty to which his rank and status is appropriate."

I was so relieved after seeing my career flash before my eyes. My rear had been saved. You don't dare tell a superior officer what you won't do and what you will do. But there comes a point in time where any man must say, "Enough. Enough of this abuse."

This put an immediate end to the mercurial confrontation.

And when Col. Clark and I left, we walked out together.

I had never met him before, but he knew all he needed to know about me from my record. In the case of all the officers assigned to the battalion, it was his job to decide who would do what. He made his decisions based on the file, which was, theoretically, our color-blind, official service record.

If Col. Clark had not arrived at that precise moment, God only knows what would have happened. But whether someone else intervened or not, I would not and could not stand for the subtle racial abuse that this brutal colonel attempted.

When you reached the point where I was in my career, assignments became very important. This was not a game; this was the real deal.

Ironically, in some ways, the Army had been training me to become a leader, to form opinions—even though expressing them required strict adherence to military culture and hierarchy.

Standing up for myself in that moment—and finding unexpected support from a senior officer—was a personal and professional breakthrough for me.

Racism sometimes comes about in subtle ways; it's harder to deal with when it's subtle. You've got three people being considered for a job, and you don't get the job. There might not be a remedy for that. It might well be that there's some good reason why you didn't get it, even though you feel that the reason is racism. But you can't prove it. Occasionally something is so blatant that you don't mind taking a gamble with your career to say, "This, I will not do, this I will not tolerate."

And, I must point out, there was never a word uttered by any of us in that room about race.

I was assigned as the battalion operations officer (S-3) and, later, as commanding officer of C Company, which were the appropriate assignments for me as a senior captain. When I finished my ground duty, I was assigned to the 3rd Infantry Division aviation detachment at Kitzingen, Bavaria, and was soon promoted to the rank of major.

•••

When Mary and I arrived in Germany, we purchased a year-old Volvo PV544, manual transmission, for $950. Mary did not know how to drive a stick, but she was a fast learner.

The company command duty was interesting and rewarding. There were 156 men in my company. The unit was mechanized infantry, which meant that we oversaw a large number of vehicles, including the M-119 track vehicle used for troop transport.

I found the year quite rewarding on several levels. In addition to the fulfillment of the ultimate duty assignment, Mary and I had the opportunity to see a great deal of Europe. One fun week of vacation we enjoyed was at Lake Chiemsee, where we took a weeklong sailing course. Another highlight of our tour was a trip to Oberammergau in the Bavarian Alps. From there we drove across the Alps and on to the French Riviera and Barcelona. We took an overnight ferry ride, car and all, to the island of Palma, Mallorca.

On another vacation, we went north to Amsterdam and continued on to Brussels.

One weekend, all of the officers in the battalion drove to Wiesbaden in central West Germany and took a day ride up the Rhine River. We went all the way to Cologne, in the fourth-largest state in Germany, going past the Lorelei statue along the river.

These excursions served to greatly enhance time away from the United States for even the most homesick of our group. One of the joys of Army life was the opportunity to, with relatively inexpensive travel, see a great deal of the world that would hardly be affordable otherwise. Being overseas also provided an opportunity to enjoy camaraderie at its best. Typically, all military personnel resided in a compound together, and our social lives were pretty much enmeshed in one another's.

It broke barriers; it formed bonds; it built the team.

•••

Army spouses rarely get the credit they deserve for enduring relocation, cultural and social challenges, financial pressures and more. Mary put up with all that and more but believes the Army was mostly good for us and our marriage.

"The military had a lot to do with our having a successful marriage," she said, "because you always lived with knowing that you could be separated for long periods. It was up to us to make good all the times that we had together. You always had to be ready to move. We had friends and neighbors in the Army who lost their husbands in airplane accidents in the Vietnam War. We were just thankful for the time that we had.

"We went to an Oktoberfest celebration in a Munich beer hall with

German bands and folks in traditional costumes. We met some Germans, and they invited us to their home a week later. They put out a spread for us that you would not believe. Not all Germans were that way. But then all Americans were not that way, either. You find a friend where you find one. In Germany, I had a girlfriend who was Japanese. One was white from Louisiana. And one was white from Georgia.

"I enjoyed Germany best of all," Mary continued, "because we had the chance to go to a lot of different places. Shopping was good. And women were free to get in the car and go bargain hunting. I discovered antique clocks in Germany. A lot of people were collecting clocks, and some of the Germans felt that American women were buying too many of them and bringing them out of the country. I contributed to their grief; I brought home at least a half-dozen myself.

"I don't see that our army life is that special. We've had a good marriage. I'm glad I married him; I saved his life. He probably feels like he saved mine, too. I've been very happy with Felker, and I would marry him again if I could. I told him, 'Let's get married again! Let's say our vows again.' He said, 'No, I've done that once already!' "

•••

Upon my return to flight status, I was assigned as operations officer for the aviation battalion for the 3rd Infantry Division located at Kitzingen Army Airfield.

The battalion was commanded by Lt. Col. Robert McDaniel; I was commander of airfield operations. We had a company of Sikorsky H-34 helicopters and a detachment of Grumman OV-1 Mohawks, along with a small section of Bell UH-1 Iroquois helicopters. We also had a unit of single-engine fixed-wing airplanes, specifically, Cessna 0-1 Bird Dogs and de Havilland DHC-2 Beavers.

During my time in the aviation battalion, we suffered two tragedies that cost the lives of three of our pilots and one observer.

One accident was with a Beaver. We were on maneuvers in West Germany, and I had watched one Beaver take off with two experienced pilots. As I turned to walk away, I heard a loud bang, looked back and the Beaver crashed not far from the end of the runway. Both pilots were killed instantly.

The second accident involved a Mohawk. A young lieutenant by the name of Jerry Waller lost an engine soon after takeoff, and he and an observer were killed in the resulting crash.

I chaired the accident investigation team. We found that the Mohawk had suffered a catastrophic engine failure shortly after takeoff from a gravel airstrip. He had climbed less than 500 feet before losing control of the aircraft. The observer, riding in the rear seat, ejected, but did so while the aircraft was in a steep left bank, thus resulting in insufficient time for his chute to deploy. The pilot did not have time to attempt an emergency ejection. Both were killed instantly.

17. MARRIED AND ALONE, PART 2: VIETNAM

After three years in Germany, I received combat orders to Vietnam in 1966.

I was given a 30-day furlough before reporting, and Mary and I returned to the United States to prepare for a lengthy—and potentially deadly—separation.

During that time, we contracted with a gentleman to build what we imagined would one day be a permanent home for us, on a plot of land that I purchased next to my parents' home. While I was fighting in Vietnam, Mary lived with my parents and supervised the completion of the house, and then furnished it.

•••

I arrived in Vietnam in the spring of 1966. After landing at Tan Son Nhut Air Base in Saigon, I was flown by helicopter to the headquarters of the 14th Aviation Battalion in the Mekong Delta.

The air was so hot and humid that I had trouble imagining that human conditions could ever be bearable. It never did get better; it only got worse.

The next morning, as I reported to battalion headquarters for further assignment, I sat all day in the battalion commander's waiting room to be greeted and be sent to my duty station in the Mekong Delta. The battalion was commanded by Lt. Col. Maddox. Maddox passed by me several times during the course of the day, never greeting me or speaking to me.

Finally, after waiting at least five hours, I was ordered to board a helicopter flight to my duty station with the 114th Aviation Company. The 114th was commanded by a major and populated by half a dozen other majors, including me. We flew UH-1A helicopters in support of South Vietnamese ground combat forces. The only other U.S. personnel in the Mekong were advisers to the South Vietnamese forces.

On my first full day with the U.S. 114th, I was assigned to fly with the platoon leader, a young captain who had been in the country approximately six months and knew the ropes.

The group making the flight with us was accompanied by four or five other helicopters armed with machine guns and rockets, which could wreak havoc on targets. At 30 minutes out, we came upon a single file of what appeared to be civilian personnel, moving across an open field. Soon, the platoon leader captain with whom I was flying ordered the other choppers in the group to open fire with their machine guns and rockets on the "civilians." But these were no ordinary civilians; they were actually enemy combatants with powerful weapons concealed under their clothing.

Those who were not killed in the open field took off running toward a clump of trees just ahead of them. Our choppers fired several rockets at the trees, triggering a series of explosions caused by munitions stockpiles concealed in the woods.

It was a sickening sight for me. I asked the platoon leader captain how he knew that this was a combat unit operating in an open field.

"You'll figure it out quickly enough," he said.

This was my first exposure to the evolving nature of guerrilla warfare, in which the opposition was not dressed in uniform, nor attacking in troop

HEADQUARTERS
UNITED STATES ARMY VIETNAM
APO San Francisco 96307

GENERAL ORDERS   16 February 1967
NUMBER   705

AWARD OF THE LEGION OF MERIT

1. TC 320. The following AWARD is announced.

WARD, FELKER W. JR. 097647 MAJOR INFANTRY United States Army,
Headquarters, United States Army Vietnam, APO 96307
Awarded: Legion of Merit
Date action: March 1966 to February 1967
Theater: Republic of Vietnam
Reason: For exceptionally meritorious conduct in the performance of
        outstanding service.
Authority: By direction of the President under the provisions of the
        Act of Congress, approved 20 July 1942, and Executive
        Order 10600, 15 March 1955.

FOR THE COMMANDER:

RICHARD J. SEITZ
Brigadier General, US Army
Chief of Staff

S. A. MacKENZIE
Colonel, AGC
Adjutant General

DISTRIBUTION:
  5 - Each unit concerned
  2 - AVHGA
  1 - AVHIG
  3 - AVHIO
  2 - AVHAG-A
 20 - AVHAG-ED
  7 - CINCUSARPAC
  2 - CINCUSARPAC ATTN: GPOP-MH

SPECIAL DISTRIBUTION:
  2 - TAGO, DA ATTN: AGPF-F
      (for official personnel file)
  1 - Dir, OPD, OPO, DA ATTN: OPIN

formation. Recognizing the enemy in Vietnam would rely as much on instinct as certainty. This was not Korea; it was certainly not the trenches of
World War II.

The Vietnam War in the Mekong Delta was fought in an unusual manner. On a day-to-day basis, we were assigned the mission of picking up
South Vietnamese personnel whom we were to support that day. We found
them in the villages where they had spent the previous night with their
families. We transported them to an area identified by map coordinates,
where they were to search for combatants. At a pre-set time, later in the
day—or upon call-on radios—we picked them up for transport back to

their village for the night. If they had serious injuries, we took them to medical facilities for care.

On one occasion, my chopper and another accompanying me were assigned the mission of transporting several senior South Vietnamese officers. Our orders were to drop them off and depart to a safe location and remain there until we were called by radio to come back in and pick them up.

As soon as we dropped them, we received frantic calls to return and rescue the officers because they were under fire. We immediately circled back and got them out to safety.

Four weeks later, the crews of both choppers reported to Vietnam Command Headquarters, where we were awarded the Vietnamese Cross of Gallantry for our deed in rescuing the South Vietnamese senior officers.

•••

Joining the 114th Aviation Company, I met Maj. Jim Mitchell, the only other African-American officer in the company. We generally hung out together during the brief time that we overlapped in Vietnam.

The Mekong Delta was always hot. Really, really hot and humid. We lived in tents covered by mosquito nets. It was not unusual to have to change sheets once or twice every 24 hours. Heavy rains—a monsoon, really—occurred about the same time every afternoon, cooling the air considerably and providing an opportunity to take a brief nap.

We did not have electricity, except for gasoline-powered generators. This presented a significant challenge in providing illumination for the flight line where our helicopters were parked. We accomplished this by firing 4.2-inch illuminating mortar rounds that, after being fired, were open parachutes and provided up to 4 minutes of ground illumination. Even though the 4.2-inch mortar firings created quite a loud noise, we became accustomed to hearing it all night long.

One night, however, while we were in the Officers Club after dinner, passing the time with a game of "Liar's Dice," we heard an accelerated frequency of the illumination rounds. We quickly realized that we were hearing *incoming* enemy mortar fire. We ran for our bunkers—but *not* before we took a few seconds to distribute the "scrip" (money) at our card table to the players. Each of us received about 30 cents from the basket. Can you believe it?

In a war with no defined position (and enemies indistinguishable from civilians) the bad guys could be anywhere and anyone—cooks in our kitchen, grounds maintenance personnel, even food delivery drivers. Delivery trucks were always in and out of our compound, and after a while, we simply didn't pay much attention to it.

On this occasion, after the noise subsided, we rushed to the flight lines and started the engines of our helicopters to move them out before they incurred much damage. (Fortunately, the incoming fire was not accurate.)

As I indicated previously, we had an abundance of senior field-grade officers in the theater, far more than the organizational tables called for. In other words, we were top-heavy in officers. The Army trained pilots, but without slots in those personnel ranks. Somehow, the Army had not planned the organizational structure for aviation units very well, and it was some years thereafter before the brass got their arms around this problem.

One day, I traveled to Saigon to do some shopping and, while walking down the street, a miracle happened. I ran into Capt. Ben Fowler, the officer who was my boss when I was stationed at Lawson Field in Fort Benning, Georgia. We were glad to see each other. He informed me that Army headquarters had an opening for an experienced aviation logistics officer and that I could fill the bill.[16] I immediately pursued the opportunity and within 24 hours received orders reassigning me to Saigon and to U.S. Army HQ.

The Army contingent in Vietnam was commanded by a three-star general, and I soon inherited the job of advising him on the distribution of replacement helicopters in the theater, as well as the priority of repair facilities.

Gen. William Westmoreland commanded all U.S. forces in Vietnam. While I was only a major at the time, I was frequently called upon to recommend distribution and replacement helicopters for the aviation units. I wound up on the general staff in Saigon; part of my responsibility was to do all that was possible to ensure the supply chain for military transport aircraft in Vietnam was functional. This task twice resulted in my having to fly back to the United States to deal with kinks in the supply system. A mission to Honolulu, Hawaii, came with an additional seven days' furlough, and Mary flew over to visit with me. It was an awesome break from the daily life in Vietnam.

At Army HQ, we worked seven days a week. Every other week, we had one day off. Our chaplain scheduled a Sunday morning service weekly. I made it my business to take time from my work to attend chapel services that were conducted in the building where we worked. When it became apparent that I would attend these services on a regular basis, several other key staff officers and eventually our commanding general also broke for prayer and reflection on Sunday mornings.

•••

Paul Karas, one of my very good friends from Fort Meade, Maryland, was stationed in Vietnam at the same time, although not in the same unit.

---

[16] Here comes God, intervening again.

Paul, who was also a helicopter pilot, came down from his duty station to visit me, and we spent a fun New Year's Eve together. On Jan. 2, Paul returned to his unit.

The next day, I received a call from our local military hospital to come and identify the remains of Paul Karas.

It happened that Paul, who was a captain at that time, had led a squadron of choppers into a landing zone to drop off a contingent of South Vietnamese troops. As it turned out, the landing zone was mined, and as they arrived, the mines were detonated. Paul's chopper, the lead aircraft, was destroyed, and Paul was killed instantly. He and his wife, Joyce, were close friends of mine and Mary's and we mourned his death.

•••

Upon the completion of my assignment in Vietnam, and receipt of orders back to the United States, I was awarded air medals for certain flying functions in Vietnam and also the Meritorious Service Medal.

I can hardly express the joy of arriving home and finding this fantastic home Mary had built and furnished. Thinking of that incredible moment still brings a smile to my face almost half a century later.

18. FORT MCPHERSON, GEORGIA

In 1967, my year of living dangerously in Vietnam was behind me and I was a lieutenant colonel assigned to Fort McPherson in Atlanta. My specific job was ensuring that the aviation logistic needs of the 3rd Army across the Southeast were met. Included was the responsibility to periodically inspect units in the Army area. I led an inspector general team (IG) through the aviation units.

On one occasion, I, along with three of my civilian deputies, elected to do an IG inspection at Fort Rucker, Alabama. We drove there in my personal car, and when we arrived it was dinnertime. We went to a popular restaurant in Dothan that was recommended to us by the local military people.

My companions and I walked up to the door, and I was personally greeted at the door.

"We are not integrated yet," the man said, blocking my entry.

Maybe "greeted" was not the right word.

I was in charge of this group of U.S. civilians, but only the whites serving under me were welcome to eat there. I was not.

"They can eat here," he said, "but you can't.

I didn't argue with the man. I simply said to my subordinates, "You guys, if you want to walk back home, feel free to eat here. The car and I are driving back to the base."

There was some grumbling from the men, but most of it was them being embarrassed by my treatment. We went back to the base and ate at the Officers Club.

It was very awkward and embarrassing for all four of us. As part of my exit report, when we had finished all of our inspections, I included this incident in my report to the commanding general and insisted that the military take action to place this restaurant officially "off limits" to soldiers until such time that management saw fit to obey the law and honor it.

The irony of it was that I was in charge of the detail, and yet purely on the basis of my skin color, I could not eat a meal with my subordinates.

Same thing happened again in Memphis, Tennessee.

I commanded an aircraft that was flying from Fort Benning to Fort Knox and we needed to refuel in Memphis. We landed, taxied in, shut down and headed to the airport restaurant while a crew refilled our plane.

At the restaurant, I was refused entry. The white officers—my subordinates—were welcome, but I was not. The only way that I would be served was around back at a to-go window.

I, of course, refused to do that.

My legal options were extremely limited in the late 1960s, despite my status as a military officer. This was their policy. But what I did do was file another written report with the nearest base commander. I indicated that it would be appropriate for him to also put that restaurant off-limits to military personnel until such time that the restaurant's management decided to open its doors and accept African-Americans.

•••

It has never been my nature to sit back and see things that are wrong and not work toward correcting them. But I wouldn't do something that didn't move the needle or simply kicked the can down the road. That's what I've done all my life.

This may surprise some people to hear but the Army—and, I'm sure, the other services as well—actually addressed many issues ahead of the rest of the society in which we live. The Civil Rights Movement was no exception.

In the decades following President Truman's Executive Order 9981 on military desegregation, the Army created new military occupation specialties—MOS's in Armyspeak—to deal with the technical aspects of integration and discrimination. It assigned commissioned officers and non-commissioned officers to administer the program. But there were two problems with that. Number one, it was a dead end, career-wise. It was not unlike being assigned to a motor pool in terms of career development. In other words, Army leadership at that time did not place much importance on this activity. And two, the only way a person could effect change in that environment was for change to come from the top down, not the bottom up. Whoever was in charge needed to embrace and endorse the effort, intent and need to change.

While the United States experienced violent racial turmoil from 1964-67, I was continuously stationed in Europe and Asia. But we were kept

DEPARTMENT OF THE ARMY

CERTIFICATE OF APPRECIATION

TO

MARY E. WARD

On the occasion of the retirement of her husband from active duty with the United States Army has earned the Army's grateful appreciation for her own unselfish, faithful and devoted service. Her unfailing support and understanding helped to make possible her husband's lasting contribution to the nation.

Given under my hand this 31ST day of MARCH 19 74

GENERAL, UNITED STATES ARMY
CHIEF OF STAFF

well-informed of what was happening back home in the Civil Rights Movement thanks to "Stars and Stripes," the military newspaper. It did a decent job of keeping soldiers aware of the broad strokes of what was happening back in the States and we had our own problems in the Army.

I recall an open forum we had of several hundred military people at Fort McPherson in 1968, following several race riots at military bases, both in the U.S. and abroad. Those in attendance could stand up and make uncensored statements about military integration and say what they felt without fear of intimidation or repercussions.

A white full colonel rose up to speak. He was nakedly critical of any effort toward equal opportunity and affirmative action. He told everyone how thankful we should be to be in America, how his family had immigrated here, that he was first generation born here, and how great an opportunity America had offered to him and his family.

He was senior to me, but it was another one of those cases where your blood rises up and you don't think about the consequences of your actions before you start talking.

I was quite upset.

I stood up and said, "Colonel, you don't have a right to tell me how I should feel about the way I'm being treated in my country. The day you arrived here, the very fact of the color of your skin meant that you had no problem and no worry with discrimination, whereas my people have been here all along. We've helped build this city and build this country, and you haven't done a thing to help with it. I don't want to hear from you about how we should look at things."

After a deafening silence, the open house ended right there on that note.

At some point in anyone's life you have to be willing to take a stand. And that colonel's speech was typical of what African-Americans encountered in the Armed Forces and everywhere else.

III. CIVILIAN LIFE

19. TO LAW SCHOOL AND BEYOND

As my time in Vietnam came to a close, I became interested in drawing an assignment to a city such as Atlanta or San Francisco, where there were good law schools and Army units. Landing back home in Atlanta and assigned back to Fort McPherson, I took the Law School Admissions Test (LSAT) and was accepted to Emory University School of Law in September 1967.

Law school was all that I had hoped it would be, and more.

My assignment at Fort McPherson was as deputy logistics officer in 3rd Army HQ. It required me to travel a fair amount, mostly conducting inspector general reviews and inspections for the aviation logistics operations of various bases within the 3rd Army's region: Georgia, Alabama, Kentucky, North Carolina, South Carolina, Tennessee and Mississippi.

Emory University had an evening division in the law school; the classes I took at the end of my daily job as a lieutenant colonel were taught by the same professors and followed the same curriculum as the day school. My professors worked with me so that if Army business caused me to miss a class, I could always make it up when I returned. In fact, if I missed a night class, I could usually catch a class the next day.

On the road, I carried my books with me, and did a great deal of work in my off-hours. The schedule I kept—Army during the days, law school at night—was extremely demanding. While I always made passing grades, they would have been better had I been a full-time student. It took four years to complete my legal education as opposed to the normal three. At that point, I was as old as most of the law professors, and indeed, became friendly with several.

•••

I distinctly remember, as if it were yesterday, April 4, 1968, the day that Dr. Martin Luther King Jr. was assassinated in Memphis. I was in Atlanta and attending law school at Emory University. The university closed down immediately, as did most city government offices and businesses.

The businesses closed out of fear. The university closed out of respect.

I was 35 by then, a husband, father, military officer and law student, and I was senior in age and life experience to almost all of the other students who were just out of college. Frankly, my peer group was more reflective of the professors than my fellow students.

Several professors, including Nathaniel Gozansky, Harold Marquis and Bill Ferguson, formed a group with the goal of moving Atlanta's integration forward. They approached Mary and me and asked if we would become associated with them in a social way, and any other way that we could be helpful.

They suggested dining as a group, one restaurant at a time, for integrated dinners across the city. No protests, no civil disobedience, just a quiet show of relationships for blacks and whites sharing meals together in adult settings.

I said, "That's fine. We'll be happy to do that."

Future Atlanta Mayor Maynard Jackson was among the city leaders to join us in making a statement.

But I didn't consider that to be much progress. We had just returned from four years overseas where black and white officers and their spouses and children ate dinner together every day. I was disappointed to know that Atlantans were so backward in our city, in our country, that going to dinner with blacks and whites at the table together was still a noteworthy event.

•••

At the point that I had advanced far enough in law school to graduate within the next year, I applied for and was accepted in the Army's "degree completion program." It permitted graduate students a year of full-time study while remaining on active military duty. It was an excellent program and facilitated my completing law school earlier than I had anticipated, in 1971. I passed the State Bar of Georgia that same year.

Meanwhile, during my last two years of active service, I was transferred to the Public Affairs Division, 3rd Army. My function was speechwriter for the most senior commanders of the 3rd Army—the commander, field commander and deputy commander. The deputy commander was Maj. Gen. George B. Pickett III. He was the descendant of a family that traced back to Confederate leaders. It was not unusual for us to engage in rambunctious discussions about the Civil War, as it was the general's position that had the South not run out of ammunition, it would have won the Civil War. My response was that they did run out of ammunition, and, therefore, did not win the Civil War. Notwithstanding our different viewpoint on history, I found it to be a pleasure preparing remarks for various occasions for Gen. Pickett as he appreciated and encouraged my point of view and my candor.

•••

The construction of Interstate highways 75, 85 and 20 caused tremendous social and cultural changes in Atlanta, destroying whole neighborhoods and ways of life.

The impact was something I noticed the first time I came home after being away for a few years. I had my car shipped back to New York from Germany and I picked it up and drove back to the Peach State. But upon arrival, I had trouble finding my way home, because they'd closed off so many streets and added massive, elevated highways. (It got worse—and better—in the 1990s as the city prepared to host the 1996 Summer Olympics.)

Another thing that I noticed was that the racial divide had shifted. When I left, there were neighborhoods that were all-white, and others that were all-black. That was no longer the case. And the colleges were integrated by then. The University of Georgia was integrated, as were Emory University, Georgia Tech and Georgia State.

There were more and more black leaders who emerged in politics, business and education while I was away. People such as my Tuskegee roommate Herman J. Russell had come into their own as business leaders while I was away. Maynard Jackson was the mayor! Jesse Hill became the first African-American to head the Atlanta Chamber of Commerce, a monumental development for the black community.

Governance—both public and private—was no longer automatically white. That was revolutionary in the city that gave birth to Dr. Martin Luther King Jr.

Our second home was in a community called Kings Forest, which is just west of Interstate 285 (and Fairburn Road) in southwest Atlanta. We were the second black family in the entire subdivision. In subdivisions all over town, the first upwardly mobile black families would move in and then most of the whites would move out. That happened in Kings Forest. It's amazing how big and fast the shift occurred. It was like a hurricane went through, but instead of uprooting trees and homes, it relocated families.

It was interesting to listen to the white families explain why they were moving; we'd gotten to know many of them.

A couple we knew explained that they were selling because they got so much more money for their house than they had paid for it.

"Oh," I said, "Is that right?"

We joined the neighborhood United Methodist Church, which was 90 percent white. A year later, it was 80 percent white. Two years later, it was 60 percent white. In our third year in Kings Forest, the church was equally divided between white and black parishioners.

Meanwhile the schools were officially integrated, but the businesses were less integrated.

In my neighborhood, Mary and I became friends with some of our white neighbors. We had done community events together such as raising our gardens. When we started building our current house, our neighbors brought us refreshments and said, "Welcome to the neighborhood!" That was a big change from a generation ago.

•••

As a career, 20 years was all I would give the Army, for a couple of reasons. Inside of me beats the heart of an avid entrepreneur. I really wanted to be involved in financial pursuits.

When I approached 20 years of service, I was working for 50 percent of my active-duty pay, because if I made $500 a month, I could get half of that in retirement. Why work full-time for half pay? There was a clear financial incentive to retire.

I could have stayed on active duty and gone into the JAG—Judge Advocate General's Corps. But it was a limited practice, whereas I wanted to be footloose and fancy free with legal opportunities.

In the military, one thing that's attractive is that everybody in a certain classification makes the same amount of money. There's no cutthroat behavior in that regard, except in terms of getting assignments. But in terms of pay, the Army was not the place to get rich.

Once I completed law school, I was ordered back to South Korea for a final active-duty assignment.

The commanding general of the 3rd Army sent a message to the commanding general of the 8th Army in South Korea that I was en route to his command and recommended that I be assigned to the Public Affairs Office. As a result of this favorable assignment, I was able to have my family accompany me on this last tour. We lived in a brand-new apartment building that housed international families, military and non-military alike.

By then Mary and I had adopted two children, our daughter, Felecia Wynette—we nicknamed her "Wende"—and our son, Felker III, "Jay." We nicknamed him "Jay" because Mary's name was Jamerson and he seemed more like her side of the family. Our children had the rich experience of attending an international elementary school in Seoul, where they met children from around the world. It was a beautiful and meaningful experience both for them and for us, making this assignment quite different from any other in my Army career. The exposure to different peoples was extraordinarily good for all of us. Seeing the world through the eyes of our children really lit up the Seoul assignment for us.

Mary worked as an assistant to a military judge in Seoul. Most of our Sundays were spent at church and on the golf course with our friends Jack and Marilyn Thompson.

Before leaving Seoul, we adopted a third child, Wesley. *(More about our children can be found in Chapter 29.)*

Upon completion of the South Korean assignment, I had six months left before retirement, which was not sufficient time for a meaningful assignment. Instead, I received what was called a "project transition" assignment, whereby I could remain on active duty and begin developing a civilian career and lifestyle.

•••

One of my classmates at Emory was Thelma Wyatt. After law school, she hung out a shingle as a solo practitioner in Atlanta.

I entered into a partnership with Thelma under the name of Ward & Wyatt.

I became active in the Gate City Bar Association, the membership of which primarily consisted of African-American lawyers in Atlanta. It was a small group at the time; there were just 10 of us in the entire city in those days. After a relatively short period of time, I was elected president of the Gate City Bar. When I discovered that the older black lawyers—genuine pioneers upon whose shoulders we stood—had become disenfranchised from the organization in terms of active practice, I made it a goal of my presidency to bring them back into the fold. That grew the size and experience level of the Gate City Bar, and everyone benefited.

Thelma was most adept at the business practice, while I was more interested in the litigation practice. It made for an excellent partnership.

Two years later, Thelma was appointed to a judgeship in the city of Atlanta. I was happy for her—although sorry to see our partnership end.

I wasn't alone for long, though.

20. THE SADDEST DAY OF MY LIFE, 1970

My last active duty assignment was Seoul, South Korea.

When Mary, the kids and I returned to the United States in 1970, we first visited Mary's sister Marion and her husband, Bob Moses. They lived in Seaside, California. Bob had retired from the Army at Fort Ord and they elected to remain in the area.

Upon arrival back in Atlanta, I wondered why my mother and dad weren't at the airport to welcome us home.

In the past, every time we left for overseas—or returned—they were there. They always made time for the big events in our family life. And so I was rather perplexed about why they were not there to meet the plane.

My cousin, James Brooks was there. He had the unfortunate job of telling us why he was alone.

"Your brother was killed yesterday," he said. "That's why your parents are not here today."

Solomon was at home in Henry County. There was a knock at his door. When he answered it, two white men shot and killed him, execution-style.

He had a wife, Christine, and a 6-year-old daughter, Crystal. They were both at home when it happened.

We never learned why someone put a hit on Solomon; I'm not so sure how professional or skilled—or even motivated—the homicide investigation unit was.

We didn't have the money to put up a high reward back in those days, so it didn't happen.

My parents were in mourning, naturally, totally shook up. In the years immediately before the shooting, my mother was in remission from breast cancer. Her health took a turn for the worse after Solomon's inexplicable and sudden death. I'm convinced that the murder of her middle son contributed greatly to her own demise.

When Solomon was murdered, it was the darkest day of my life, because I lost not only a brother, but my best friend.

My brother was a better athlete than I, even though he was three years younger—a better pitcher and better hitter, to be specific.

There were times when I had to play the older brother role in his life. But that's only because we were close and shared so much, good times and bad.

My brother was always good with animals. I think they could sense what a gentle soul he was. My brother could walk up to a dog that would attack you or me, but the dog wouldn't thinking of going after him. He'd put his hand on the dog's head and soothe the creature.

The other immediate effect that Solomon's death had on our family was that Mary and I shook up our future plans. We had planned to settle in Tampa, Florida, when I retired from the Army and finished law school. I had passed the Florida Bar and received an offer from one of the biggest law firms in Florida to join them as a partner.

But when Solomon died, my mother and dad needed me in Atlanta to help them through this horrific trauma. We had even bought some waterfront land on which to build a new home, but we put off moving to Florida. Instead, I began establishing myself in the city of Atlanta. Picking up and moving without losing ground is not as easy as you might think. It became harder and harder as time went by for me to break away and fulfill our dream of living in the Sunshine State.

21. PUBLIC SERVICE, PUBLIC LIFE

One characteristic that flows through my life is that I've always been interested in serving. And I've never been a member of an organization of which I didn't wind up leading.

When Maynard H. Jackson was elected mayor of Atlanta in 1973, it was a big deal. An African-American running City Hall? In Atlanta? Few of us ever thought we'd see that happen in our lifetimes. But Jackson went on to serve back-to-back terms, leading the city through 1980. He was followed by Andrew Young, after his historic service as the U.S. ambassador to the United Nations under President Jimmy Carter. (Jackson returned to the office for a third term in 1990.)

There was a lot of good in Maynard Jackson's eight years in office during the 1970s. But it was somewhat blemished by a police scandal that occurred on his watch, one that eventually drew me in.

A. Reginald Eaves, also African-American, was the public safety commissioner under Jackson, the first African-American in that role. Jackson took aggressive steps to bring African-American police officers to the force and Eaves carried out the mayor's policies. The ranks of the Atlanta police department were totally out of balance with the racial makeup of our city. Even once African-Americans started wearing blue, there were still only a few of them in the rank of sergeant or higher.

Eaves desperately wanted to correct this situation.

Eaves gave birth to the idea of making an examination prematurely available to eight African-American officers who were up for promotion. He chose his driver to distribute the exam.

When Mayor Jackson learned of this breach, he appointed a two-

Mary, left, and Felker Ward Jr. hosted a re-election campaign event in support of Atlanta Mayor Maynard Jackson, center. Also pictured is the Rev. Reynell Parkins.

member commission to study the charges and to give him a report on their findings. He selected a high-profile white Republican of great national esteem. Randolph Thrower was known in Atlanta as a partner at the law firm of Sutherland Asbill & Brennan LLP, but across the country, he was recognized as the defiant head of the Internal Revenue Service from 1969-71 under then President Richard M. Nixon. Thrower lost his job for resisting the president's demand that he punish Nixon's enemies via tax audits.

I was asked to work alongside Thrower as co-chair of the mayor's commission—I as an African-American Democrat almost 20 years his junior.

It was my first high-profile civic assignment since leaving the Army and it lasted six months. At times, Thrower and I worked seven days a week. We interviewed more than 100 police officers, ordering polygraph tests of many of them as we investigated the practices of the Atlanta police department. Mayor Jackson granted us subpoena power and we took testimony with appropriate sanctions for lying under oath.

At the conclusion of our work, we reported to the mayor that, indeed, the exam had been compromised and made available to these officers in advance, and six of the eight admitted, ultimately, that they did have the exam.

For the six who admitted their complicity, we recommended to the mayor that they be rolled back to their previous rank. For the other two, we found them guilty of lying under oath and recommended that punitive action be taken against them. (As for Eaves, he resigned in 1978 under threat of being fired by Mayor Jackson, although he wasn't out of the public eye long. That same year, he won election to the Fulton County Board of Commissioners, where he served for the next decade.)

•••

Georgia Gov. George Busbee (1975-83), appointed my friend, African-American civil rights attorney and Georgia state legislator William A. "Bill" Alexander to the bench of the Fulton County Court.

Alexander was previously a member of the state's General Assembly and he asked me to attend the swearing-in ceremony and formally present him for his ordination. I gladly did so and, in my remarks, made the point of stressing how significant it was that Gov. Busbee had appointed the first African-American to a judgeship in Fulton County.

I became acquainted with the governor that way. And Alexander's seat was now open. I'd just retired from the Army and I thought that running for office might be a way of continuing to serve.

Well, nine other people felt the same way.

A total of 10 of us ran for the seat vacated by Alexander.

I came in fourth.

The three people ahead of me had previously run for public office. They had high name recognition. Most of the six behind me were well-known in the city. I was glad I ran, because it was enough to let me know that I did not want to hold public office. It cured me forever of that disease.

Later, several members of the Fulton County Commission got themselves in trouble, and they had to be replaced. Gov. Busbee was to appoint their replacements. He offered me one of the seats. I turned to Charlie Weltner and Marvin S. Arrington for advice.

"Felker," Arrington said, "whatever you do, don't take that appointment. You've just started a law practice. You're doing well. Stay focused on that. Because the very first thing that will happen is you will get this appointment and a client will need your help on a day when there's a flag pole being dedicated somewhere, and you're expected to be there for it."

Weltner gave me the same advice. I took it and passed on politics.

•••

The same day as the Alexander appointment, the governor sent Tom Perdue and Tom Daniel to meet with me and offer me a position on the Georgia Judicial Nominating Commission. This commission had a tremendous responsibility ahead of it in upgrading and diversifying the Georgia judiciary.

If a lawyer or other citizen wanted to become a judge—or was already a judge and wanted to step up to a higher court—his or her application was submitted to this commission. It was comprised of the state's attorney general, the chief justice of the Supreme Court, the Georgia Bar president, the Georgia Bar past-president, the Georgia Bar president-elect and three or four others. In addition, there were three or four slots filled by the governor's own appointments, and I was one of those.

It was a great introduction for me to the Georgia judiciary and the state bar as a whole. One of my fellow commission members was W. Stell Huie, then the president of the State Bar of Georgia. Service on the Judicial Nominating Commission was demanding and time-intensive, as we thoroughly reviewed the applications of all who were interested in becoming a judge. Not only did we have to examine their records, we also conducted a lengthy personal interview with each applicant. In the course of this work, Stell and I became acquainted.

Stell invited me to lunch at the Commerce Club. I accepted, and Stell presented me with another invitation: to become a partner in his law firm. Founded by Bob Kutak in 1965 in Omaha, Nebraska, Kutak Rock & Huie had offices in Omaha, Atlanta, Denver and Washington, D.C. Its national presence was exciting, and I eagerly accepted.

Felker Ward Jr. being in sworn in by Georgia Gov. George Busbee as a member of the Georgia Judicial Nominating Commission.

I progressed quickly and was elected managing partner of the Atlanta office, making me the senior lawyer in the Atlanta office, and giving me a seat on the firm's national governance committee. At that time, the 50 largest law firms in America had a total of 12 black partners. Kutak had two of the 12, myself and Yvonne Brathwaite Burke, recently elected to the U.S. House of Representatives from Los Angeles.

•••

Over the next few years, there were several occasions when I was able to provide public service.

And one that I declined: I was approached about being nominated to be a judge myself on the Georgia Supreme Court. I chose to pass, primarily for economic reasons.

•••

In addition to my continuing position on Georgia's Judicial Nominating Commission, Gov. Joe Frank Harris asked me to head up a biracial committee to understand the causes of a 1987 Ku Klux Klan attack in Forsyth County, Georgia, that ended in violence—and to find ways of alleviating the immense amount of ill will in that county.

Racial strife in Forsyth County—1987 population of 38,000 and located 40 miles north of Atlanta—dated back to 1912. According to "Report of the Cumming/Forsyth County Biracial Committee" (Dec. 22, 1987):

"During the month of September 1912, a white Forsyth County teenager was murdered and raped. Three black men were charged with this crime. One alleged accomplice, a black man, was shot in the Forsyth County jail. The Sheriff of Forsyth County during the fall of 1912 sought the help of the state militia and secreted the other charged blacks to Atlanta for protection pending trial. The accounts of these events received nationwide publicity. In the trial, a sister of one of the three charged men implicated the three by her testimony. The remaining two were convicted and hanged, at sentence of court, just west of the present Courthouse square in Cumming. Executions were carried out in the county of trial at that time. This law was changed not many years after these events.

"Following 1912, the black population of Forsyth County diminished rapidly and virtually ceased to exist by the time of the Great Depression ...

"In early January of 1987, a small group of white residents of Forsyth County, and Hall County, sought to organize in Forsyth County, what was styled as a "Brotherhood March." Coincidentally, the march was to have occurred at the time of the annual King birthday celebrations. Due to considerable controversy, the original organizers cancelled their initial plans, partially as a result of threats and intimidation. Subsequently, plans for the 'Brotherhood March' were taken up by a white Hall County resident named Dean Carter. Mr. Carter invited various Civil Rights leaders and organizations to participate in the proposed 'Brotherhood

Gov. Joe Frank Harris appointed Felker Walter Jr. as chairman, along with other members of the newly established Georgia Human Relations Commission.

March.' On January 17, 1987, a group of approximately 45 persons from Atlanta joined approximately 30 persons from the Forsyth and Hall County areas on a county road in in south Forsyth County. This group was met by approximately 400 spectators and white supremacist group members from various locations. During this march, violence occurred by method of jeering, heckling, preprinted signs with racist slogans, thrown rocks, mud and bottles. National media coverage escalated the controversy and conflicts surrounding the event.

"As a result of the initial march on January 17, 1987, a hastily organized consortium of various Civil Rights organizations was formed, and became known as the Coalition to End Fear and Intimidation in Forsyth County. This group made efforts to conduct a second 'Brotherhood March' on January 24, 1987. Although the magnitude of the second 'Brotherhood March' was unknown to this group, approximately 25,000 marchers from locations throughout the United States, converged on Cumming/Forsyth County on January 24, 1987 ..."

The second march attracted thousands of people, myself included. Organized busloads of us came up from Atlanta, as did people from all over the country. That, of course, drew hundreds of law enforcement officials. It was incredibly tense, but the march went off without incident. It was mostly peaceful. However, not much was accomplished other than putting a spotlight on this race-driven county. It soon became clear that whites—including the Klan—enjoyed full support in Forsyth County.

The governor, Joe Frank Harris, got involved after the second march. He asked me if I would lead an African-American delegation (including Daisy Bailey, William Bauman, Janet Douglas, Dr. Major Jones and Elisabeth Omilami) representing The Coalition to End Fear and Intimidation in Forsyth County. He matched me up with white attorney Phill Bettis, representing Forsyth County (along with white committee members James G. Harris, Charles Ingram, the Rev. Harold Lawrence, the Rev. John Lummus and Charles R. Smith), and we were charged with trying to make some progress in terms of race relations there.

We met every two weeks at the courthouse in Cumming and worked together on issues of repatriation, fair housing practices, equal employment opportunities and more for the next 10 months.

We recognized that those who commit such horrific acts don't operate in the daylight. They only come out in darkness—like cockroaches. Still, we were never there at night. We always went up in the light of day and left before night fell.

Every time we went to Forsyth County for a meeting, Sheriff Wesley C. Walraven Jr. sent armed deputies in unmarked cars to meet us at the county line and escort us to the courthouse. When each meeting was over, they escorted us back out of the county. Their presence ensured nothing bad happened to us, and we appreciated it.

When we started our inquiry, the Forsyth County entourage was immediately on the defensive.

The first meeting I convened got off to a fairly rocky start. The Forsyth contingent contended that the troublemakers during the first march were not Forsyth County citizens, but rather Ku Klux Klansmen, 13 of them from outside of the county.

My response was that it seemed difficult to imagine that 13 Ku Klux Klansmen from outside of the county could take charge and be responsible for the conduct of a large group of local citizens in Forsyth County whom they had never before met. That was ground zero of our later discussions.

I said, "I find it difficult to believe that you were that helpless."

As if it happened randomly, that the Klan had a meeting and someone said, "Hey, I've got an idea! Let's stir up trouble in Forsyth County! I know where they keep the keys to the jail!"

We went on to meet for 10 months, talking about specific steps that could be taken to help break the social and cultural logjam there.

We worked well alongside Bettis. Our goal was to not just get to the bottom of the violence but to offer constructive solutions going forward.

One of the things we talked about was jobs and one of the methods we used to try to make sense of what happened in that area was to encourage contractors to hire outside of the county and employ African-American workers. That was a challenge because black people said, "We can't get caught in Forsyth County at night." Our idea was that the sheriff hire one or more African-Americans to work in law enforcement.

Another issue that we touched on but never reached a satisfactory solution on was land ownership. In those days, what happened frequently across the South was that taxes would be raised so high on property that African-Americans couldn't pay it. Whites would go in and pay the back taxes on black-owned property—and, after a period of time, they had enough invested in it to where they could petition the court and take ownership, pushing black families out. It might have been legal, technically, but totally immoral and un-Christian. In the years and decades since then, real estate values in Cumming have grown exponentially. Forsyth County is one of the fastest-growing counties in the entire United States. And so those properties, if those African-American families had held them, would be quite valuable.

A major highway—Georgia 400—runs from Atlanta north right through the heart of Forsyth County. And when the county started to grow by leaps and bounds, developers and real estate moguls paid a big price for property along that highway with the idea that Fortune 500 companies were beginning to move headquarters into the Atlanta area and would be attracted to nearby Forsyth County.

But the attitude of corporate investors of the world was, "We will not invest in a county with that kind of racial tension." The investors who had bought up land on spec became nervous and concerned. They called and asked if I would meet with them. I did. The essence of the meeting was, "Whatever you tell us we've got to do, that's what we will do. We cannot afford to lose the money we invested." They were less motivated by fighting racism than saving their investments, but the effect was the same.

I encouraged them to do the same as I did the sheriff: reach out and find ways to employ African-Americans in Forsyth County; make it worth their while to work there and ensure their safety—day and night. If that worked, blacks would slowly but surely start migrating back.

Unfortunately, Forsyth County's white real estate agents and brokers of that era made money off of the fear of blacks that they put into other whites. For example, the neighborhood where my wife and I lived, south of Atlanta, was all-white before we bought our home and property. We were the second black family there. When more black families started moving in, the white families started moving out. And what started out as 85 percent white, wound up being less than 10 percent white, and eventually zero. That's just the way it unfolded in my neighborhood and elsewhere as African-American families moved up the socio-economic ladder in the 1970s and '80s. The main culprits were real estate agents, because they actually went door to door to intimidate white families and said, "The blacks are moving in (only they didn't use the word 'blacks') and if you don't want your property values going down, you need to sell *now*."

People cater to activities that enhance their pocketbooks, especially when it comes to real estate values. We enlisted the help of a Forsyth County real estate broker who was willing to go out of his way to try to attract African-Americans.

In any city—and Atlanta is no exception to this—if a new person comes into a city and they retain a broker to help them find a house, if the person is white, the broker send them one way; if he's black, he'll point in the opposite direction. It's very, very noticeable and it goes on every day.

I have seen so much of these things in my lifetime that it doesn't surprise me anymore. Racism can be overt, but more often the worst of it operates below the surface where it can be harder to identify and root out. At the same time, it doesn't mean that we buy into it. It means that we fight the battle in a different way.

At the end of 10 months of meetings and investigation, Bettis and I presented a forward-looking plan, "Report of the Cumming/Forsyth County Biracial Committee" (Dec. 22, 1987), to Gov. Harris. There were things we agreed upon and others we did not, which explains why the report is actually five separate reports:

• Position papers of Cumming/Forsyth County Community Relations Committee

• Position papers of Representatives of Coalition to End Fear and Intimidation in Forsyth County

• Report by Attorney General Michael J. Bowers

• Conclusions to Report submitted by Phill Bettis, Chairman, Cumming/Forsyth County Community Relations Committee

• Conclusions to report submitted by Felker W. Ward Jr., Chairman, Representatives of Coalition to End Fear and Intimidation in Forsyth County

Here are the conclusions that I offered in my final report to Gov. Harris:

"Rarely are absolutes derived from endeavors of this sort. Even the most noble efforts are seldom 100 percent successful, nor frivolous undertakings total failures.

"As one reviews this brief summary of these proceedings—which involve approximately 600 joint hours of aggregate time of 12 or more people over a period of eight months, in addition to an equal number of hours of subcommittee meetings—it is apparent that the project bears more indices of success than failure. The position papers prepared by the various members of the Bi-Racial Committee contain some conclusions. In addition the following general conclusions are offered:

"First, in most communities, including Forsyth County, there are many people of goodwill, but there are also persons of illwill *(sic)* whose influence, if unabated, will far exceed proportionately their numbers in the community. Little, if any good is achieved by blaming outsiders and the news media for problems in a community. The principles of self government embodied in our Constitution demand that the community acting jointly and through its elected officials, observe and preserve the human and civil rights of all persons who live, work in or visit the community.

"Second, during the course of these proceedings, it was apparent that some local citizens of goodwill, including some who served on this Committee, were intimidated in their efforts to disavow and to contain the persons and forces of illwill *(sic)* in the community, particularly the members of the Klan and other hate groups whose aims and purposes were and continue to be the fostering of racial strife. One is reminded of the truism that anarchy left unchecked knows no bounds and will ultimately turn not only on its initial targets, but on those who permit anarchy to flourish on the premise that it is aimed at others.

"Third, Forsyth County will never be the same again. Notwithstanding the perhaps slow and deliberate pace of change for the better, change has come and will surely continue. The events of January 1987, while not the sole motivation nor the initiating force for some of this change, will certainly have contributed to the pace of change and, to that extent, that will have been a force for good.

"Finally, Forsyth County has the opportunity to seize upon the focus which has been brought upon it. This community can demonstrate to the rest of Georgia and indeed to the world, that illwill *(sic)*, racism and anarchy can be decisively uprooted by superior forces of good in the community. It is sincerely hoped that a look back at Forsyth County in the not too distant future, will see a community which has benefited from the spotlight that was focused upon it in 1987."

At the conclusion of our work, Mary and I invited the delegation from Forsyth County—as well as the Atlanta contingent—to our home in Atlanta. They rented a bus and, I believe, enjoyed a pleasant evening with us. We went from one extreme to another in a matter of six months. That, in and of itself, was a remarkable development.

I've always dealt with these matters in a way that I would expect to win the battle and the war, to bring about change. Jumping up and down in today's world, making a lot of noise, is not always the best or only weapon a minority businessperson can call upon. There are economic weapons; there are political weapons.

Think about how the Civil Rights Movement started with a black seamstress all alone on a city bus, refusing the driver's demand that she give up her seat to a white person. Rosa Parks didn't jump up and down and scream. She simply said, "No. I will not." When the driver said, "I will have you arrested," she told him that he could certainly do that. He called the police and two officers entered the bus. They couldn't understand why Mrs. Parks refused the bus driver's instructions to yield to a white person and did, in fact, arrest her.[17]

That's sometimes how meaningful change takes place.

•••

In Forsyth County there was a fellow who produced lawn and garden products, such as topsoil and decorative bark. He wanted to sell the company. A friend of mine, with whom I shared ownership of an airplane, heard about this company for sale and asked me if I'd be interested in going in on it with him. My friend and the owner negotiated a purchase price and had a closing. Until that day, I never set foot on the property, never visited the company. Never showed my face at all. The day we closed, I went to the company headquarters in Forsyth County for the first time. Imagine us introducing ourselves to 50 or 60 employees. That's how I dealt with things like that. It was a good purchase, by the way. When we eventually sold the business, I retained an interest in the real estate in

---

[17] Source: http://teacher.scholastic.com/rosa/interview.htm#brave

which the company operated.

•••

Another racial incident occurred in Georgia in spring 1980, this time in Wrightsville, and African-American residents protested overt racist treatment. Emotions ran high and shots were fired at state patrol cars in the county.

For the second time, Gov. Harris asked if I would represent him this time in rural Johnson County and assess what needed to be done to bring peace and tranquility back to the region.

Harris dispatched Tom Perdue, Tom Daniel and me on this mission. We started with a community meeting in Wrightsville, open to the public. To succeed in the town hall type of meeting, I knew that we needed the support of Wrightsville's white leadership. In rural Georgia at that time—and probably still today—the county sheriff was the most influential person in the county. In Johnson County, it was Roland Attaway. I went to him and directly asked for his support. Attaway ran Johnson County for a quarter of a century, 1960-85, and I was told that there was no way he would support our commission, but I insisted upon a meeting anyway.

On the day that we were to meet, I drove to Wrightsville and was ushered into Sheriff Attaway's office. It was an inauspicious start for a black man; the walls were covered in Confederate paraphernalia. I was thrown back a hundred years in Southern history to a time when whites ruled with an iron thumb and blacks had few, if any, rights.

The sheriff confidently told me that "the good black folks" in Johnson County were "happy" with the way things were, that it was the outside agitators from elsewhere who were causing problems and stirring up trouble.

I, in turn, told Sheriff Attaway that the way to quell racial strife was for the local leadership—particularly him—to recognize and acknowledge the problems and to take charge and be responsible for dealing with genuine racial issues in the city.

"That way," I said, "you will not have the problem of outsiders coming in and telling you how to run your county." (In football, that's called a "draw" play.)

After a long pause, the sheriff picked up the telephone, called the county commission, directed them to cooperate with us and attend our meeting that night.

That was all we needed to get started.

The community meeting at what was then Johnson County High School drew a crowd. I believe a large majority of the county's citizens attended. The situation had reached a point that everyone knew about it. It required a solution before something worse occurred.

The population split was apparent from where I stood onstage; blacks sat on one side of the room, whites sat opposite them.

Before getting down to the business at hand, we "integrated" Johnson County by having every other row swap sides in the room. To everyone's surprise, nothing went wrong—everyone stayed cool; tempers remained in check.

During the course of the evening, with blacks and whites alike standing up and stating their concerns, we discovered that Johnson County government had only two black employees. One was an ambulance driver, and I do not recall what the other one did.

The complaints we heard were about jobs, governance, law enforcement, educational institutions and business, all of which excluded African-Americans residents of the county.

Committees were formed that night, with black and white representation on each. They were mandated to roll up their sleeves and work things out in a way that everybody would receive a fair shake.

The initiative was very successful, and today, Johnson County is thriving once more.

•••

Having established a lasting rapport with Gov. Harris, I asked for and received an appointment to the Board of Natural Resources, which was involved with things that I was personally interested in, such as outdoor life—sporting, hunting and fishing. The governor readily obliged.

The Board of Natural Resources consists of 19 citizens appointed by the governor and confirmed by the state senate. It is responsible for setting rules and regulations ranging from air and water quality to hunting rules and regulations. It has to do with game management, state parks, environmental protection—all that comes under that board. Being on it broadened the base of people who knew me, and whom I knew.

I ultimately served on the board for 17 years, including a stint as its chairman.

During my time on the board, Joe Tanner—who was the commissioner for most of those years—and I became well-acquainted. We both had boys about the same age, and we had a wonderful time deer hunting and camping together with our sons.

22. BOARDS OF HIGHER EDUCATION

In 1985, I was elected to the board of Oglethorpe University. Manning Pattillo was the university's president at the time, and one of the senior board members was Charles L. Weltner, chief justice of the Georgia Supreme Court.

Two years after that I was also approached about joining the Board of Trustees of Emory University. I responded that I was, of course, pleased about this overture, but that I couldn't do it.

"I'd like to," I said, "but I can't because I'm already on the board of Oglethorpe."

Two days later, my phone rang.

"Felker, this is Jim."

I recognized his voice, and I also knew why he was calling. But I didn't let on.

"Jim ...?"

"Jim Laney."

James T. Laney became president of Emory University in 1977 and continued in the role until 1993, when he became the U.S. ambassador to South Korea under President Bill Clinton. The school subsequently honored him by naming him president emeritus and renaming its school of graduate studies for him.

"Hey, Jim! How you doing?"

"Fine, fine. I hear that you can't come on the Emory board?"

He explained that Oglethorpe and Emory were not competing for the same students, that there was no conflict between the two institutions. Besides, I was an Emory alumnus.

"We really need you to come on the board," he said.

I promised Jim that I would think about the matter and call him back.

Over the next few days, I spent a great deal of time considering the opportunity. It was not possible, as a boy in the 1940s, for me to ever imagine that I would be part of this storied institution's governing body.

By this time I had already begun serving as an adjunct professor at Emory Law, teaching a course in civil procedure.

Having cleared up any possibility of a conflict of interest, I accepted the invitation and served with great enthusiasm until I turned 70, which was the age at which they required board members to step down. I accepted an emeritus designation, which I still hold.

Marvin S. Arrington was the only other African-American who served on the Emory board alongside me. Arrington grew up in Atlanta and also earned his law degree at Emory. He and our friend Clarence Cooper, in fact, were the very first African-American law students at Emory. Arrington served on the Atlanta City Council for more than 25 years.

He and I were called upon on several occasions for counsel regarding race issues that had arisen on the Emory campus, but other social issues as well. One that we tackled was same-sex marriage.

A same-sex couple applied for approval to have their marriage ceremony conducted in one of the chapels on the Emory campus. The Rev. Susan Henry-Crowe, who was at the time dean of the Chapel and Religious Life at Emory, was inclined to approve the request. The basis of her decision was that the school's chapels were non-denominational.

Even while recognizing the significant and influential role of the United Methodist Church as it related to Emory, the Rev. Henry-Crowe's position was that several denominations were recognized on campus, and if one of these denominations honored same-sex marriage, they should be permitted to conduct the ceremony on campus. The United Methodist Church was well-represented on Emory's board of trustees by several bishops who expressed concern about the matter. It was a highly inflammatory issue, and it drew a great deal of local press.

Ultimately, the board voted to permit the marriage.[18]

(The Rev. Henry-Crowe was still engaged in the national debate over same-sex marriage as recently as June 2015. As top executive of the United Methodist Board of Church and Society, she was asked for a comment when the U.S. Supreme Court established, in *Obergefell v. Hodges*, same-sex marriage as a constitutional right. In a story for the United Methodist Church's online news service, she said, "Civil society must ensure these equal protections for every person under the law. The General Board of Church and Society affirms and upholds in prayer the work of The

---

[18] As a side note, it turned out that the couple decided not to get married after all.

United Methodist Church as it continues to discern its understanding of marriage. As a denomination with members in many countries and cultures, we are thankful for all nations where religious liberty allows for the freedom for all persons to live out their faith together according to their conscience.")

•••

In 1996, while still serving on the Emory board, I received the prestigious Emory Medal, which is the highest award presented by the Emory University Alumni Association.

My audience on the day that the award was presented was the leadership of Emory University.

Here's what I said:

> *"Emory ... only in America could this happen. When I was a kid, my dad used to raise hogs. And back in those days, you could feed hogs with the waste from the cafeterias and restaurants, which is called slop. You could feed slop to the hogs. And one of the main cafeterias at Emory University was on my dad's route, his slop route. He had certain places, twice a week, he'd go on his truck with 55-gallon drums and pick up the waste that was part of his route. I used to ride with him to pick up slop, as a kid. I noticed these 100-year-old trees and these marble staircases and the beautiful, well-manicured lawns. And I remember going down one street on campus. There were signs out front with writing on it that we couldn't figure out what it was. My father said, 'My God, this looks like Greek.' We later learned that was exactly what it was. It was Fraternity Row. But never in my wildest dreams did I believe ... did I think the day would come that I'd be standing before you, a decision-maker in terms of what goes and what doesn't go in this university, that in one generation would I be here. I was not able to envision that. I think my dad was foresighted enough to see the possibility. But only in America could this happen. In any other country, it couldn't."*

I was the first—and only, to date—black to receive the honor.

23. THE PRACTICE AND THE BUSINESS THAT FOLLOWED

When Thelma and I were law partners, whatever walked in the door, that's what we practiced.

When I joined Kutak Rock & Huie, the firm was pre-eminent in the area of municipal finance. If you mentioned Kutak Rock anywhere in America at the time, its name was synonymous with municipal finance. We had 120 attorneys and were a cutting-edge firm in that area.

I, however, knew very little about municipal finance. It didn't take long for me to learn how the financial advisory and municipal finance system worked.

The year that I joined the firm, *The National Law Journal* published an article[19] that said of the 50 largest law firms in America, there were just 12 black partners among them. Kutak Rock had two of them. The law firms responded to their biggest clients, which—until then—were not interested in seeing African-Americans advance, so the law firms didn't need them. When the clients started getting interested in it, all of a sudden the law firms were interested. One followed the other.

When I first joined, I was still practicing law, but when I was elected managing partner, that was a management position. I did that for three years, but then I wanted to get back to the practice and get out of management, so I did.

•••

---

[19] "Law Journal Survey of 50 Largest Firms: 3,700 Partners, 12 Are Black," *National Law Journal*, by Edward J. Burke, July 2, 1979

I'm basically an entrepreneur. And the practice of law is a business. But you have to limit yourself to the business of practicing law.

I wanted to be a businessman beyond the business of practicing law. So in 1988, I resigned from the firm. Then I turned around and hired the firm to provide legal services for my investment management practice.

The business of municipal finance was learning to follow the money. You have to learn the regulations of municipal finance business. It's a similar set of rules for lawyers and underwriters. The difference is, as a lawyer, you're donating your time for compensation, whereas if you're an underwriter, you're investing your money for a return. Same deal, same project, different reward. I enjoyed the underwriter role and accepted the inherent risks for many years.

Eventually, however, municipal finance became mired in regulatory red tape and the risk outstripped the rewards. It was time to move on again.

About that time, Concessions International got cranked up.

24. BREAKING INTO THE WHITE COUNTRY CLUBS OF ATLANTA, BUT AT WHAT COST?

There were three private country clubs in Atlanta during the late 1970s. Most cities of our size have one or two. We had three, each one completely segregated. No African-Americans, no Jews. In my role as a leader of the Gate City Bar and the Georgia State Bar, I was involved in conversation from time to time about this situation.

On one such occasion, we met with a group comprised of the president of Emory University, the president of the State Bar of Georgia, the chief justice of the Georgia Supreme Court, and the adjutant general of the state. The leadership of all the legal entities participated in that discussion.

The object of the meeting was to enhance the citizens' view of the legal profession in Georgia.

After a full day of wide-ranging debate and discussion about what we could do in the legal profession to enhance the view that the world has of us, I said, "There's one thing that y'all have not touched on that the legal profession can do that would have a dynamic effect. Every lawyer who is a member of the Cherokee Club, the Piedmont Driving Club or the Capital City Club could come together and say, 'We insist that these clubs become integrated or we're going to pull out and create our own.' "

I paused to let the idea sink in, and then continued.

"They would be integrated, literally, in a matter of days, if not hours."

The legal representation in those clubs was so pervasive that their potential withdrawal—and the bad press it would bring—would mean that the clubs would not survive.

After I made my proposal, there was hardly any reaction among my white counterparts, except groans. In the moment, I think they were more inclined to hold bake sales for the NAACP than to unilaterally demand the clubs integrate.

But within a few days, I received private calls from several of these same legal leaders. They wanted to meet again. We made a date, and they came over to see me—I had a pretty good idea of why.

On the appointed day, one of the men came right out with a counter-proposal:

"We want to sponsor you in the Capital City Club."

"Okay," I said, "I'll consider it. And by the way, how much are the initiation fees?"

"$40,000."

If your response is that $40,000 is a lot of money, think about how much that would be in 2018 dollars—$97,344.13!

Two African-Americans were ultimately sponsored for membership in the Capital City Club in a short period of time, my college roommate, Herman J. Russell—sponsored by his longtime friend and frequent business partner, Bob Holder—and myself, sponsored by Clay Long and Manning Pattillo.

I said to the delegation, "You guys aren't as smart as I thought you were. If you were to advertise that the membership was open and the admission fee was $40,000, you still wouldn't have any more African-American members than you have right now. Nobody in their right mind will pay $40,000 for it!"

My idea was to break down the barrier, not to crawl into the space alone, so we went in, Herman and I, together. And we each dug deep and paid the price of initiation.

I was trapped, of course, and they knew it. Having been the one that raised the issue, I had no choice but to join. But as it turned out, I was glad I did. I feel that I got $40,000 worth of benefits out of it. It was a great club to be a part of.

There were many times when the only black faces in the club were Herman and me … and the men and women who worked at the club. The African-American employees were surprised to see us at first. I think some of them were nervous about it. A few were happy. You could feel it whenever Herman or I went in to order dinner or a drink; this was a new paradigm for the African-American employees.

I've run into that same feeling when I have been invited to a private plantation for hunting.

On one occasion I was invited to a plantation in Albany, Georgia. As was the case in the Capital City Club, the men and women who waited on us, prepared our meals, turned the covers back on the bed and did everything that we needed there, were African-American. It was clear to me that my presence there as an invited guest was not an everyday event for those people.

I thought I would make them comfortable by letting them know that I considered myself one of them. I wandered in the kitchen to say hello. I was immediately informed by one of the workers, "Guests are not supposed to go in our kitchen." I left and didn't go back.

In joining the Capital City Club, I was conscious of being new and different, as was my wife, Mary. But I paid my $40,000 and I wasn't concerned about whether we would get the appropriate care and treatment. After we got in, I can't tell you how many times Mary and I would be there with another couple for a meal or an event, and white men and women we knew would come over to our table to make sure that we knew how happy they were that we were there.

There were no incidents, no undertones of being unwelcome. By this time, remember, I'd spent 20 years in the Army, which is a majority white leadership atmosphere, so I was accustomed to it.

That said, I'm not naïve enough to think that every member of the club was happy that we were there.

The Capital City Club never did become broadly integrated. The initiation fee, as of 2016, reached $60,000 or more.

I applied for membership at a second exclusive club, by the way, the Piedmont Driving Club, because its golf course was more convenient for me. I was accepted. Not that anything so exclusive is that simple: I had to have at least 25 letters of recommendation from members to be considered in either one of those clubs. I had a sponsor at the Driving Club, Bob Watkins—a fellow member and friend through Rotary Club—who said, "I'm sponsoring you, and I'll get the letters you need."

Watkins gave me a book of the membership of the club. He said, "Look through this and pick out 25 or so members that I should reach out to." That's the way it works: the person who sponsors you must be someone who can influence others to help come aboard and support you.

Watkins followed through and it was done.

In 2015, after decades of membership, I resigned from the Capital City Club. I was paying for membership dues to two clubs. I didn't need but one of them, and the one I favored was the Piedmont because of its proximity to our home. It was interesting that where I moved in and helped break down a barrier, my presence there was no longer needed for any purpose other than my convenience.

The short-term purpose of integrating a civic or social group—or even the military—is not really why we do it. We're beyond that. When I was involved in integrating things like the military officers' corps, there might be 30 couples in a group and two of them would be African-American. We made it our business not to associate exclusively with each other. The reason was so that it would not appear as if we were uncomfortable or whatever within the larger group. The unspoken motive for us was, "Let's integrate this thing and not segregate ourselves."

There came a point in time where we got beyond that.

Now, if I'm at an event in a group of 25 couples and if four of them are black, I'm happy for the four of us to sit together or to dine together. We're beyond that level of having to prove, or becoming part of the group. You might say we've come full circle—at least in certain circles. In others, there is always work left to do.

From left: Felker Ward Jr., Herman J. Russell, Jesse Hill. (Photo by Horace Henry)

25. CONCESSIONS INTERNATIONAL TAKES FLIGHT

When Maynard H. Jackson was elected mayor of Atlanta, one of his major goals was providing greater access for minority and small-business enterprises to participate in city government's largest business contracts. City contracts had been dominated by white businessmen since the city was founded in 1847, and Jackson announced it was time to try something new.

One of the major projects that he inherited as mayor was the significant expansion of William B. Hartsfield Atlanta Airport (later renamed Hartsfield-Jackson International Airport to share credit between its original and modern political architects and advocates). The initiative was vigorously opposed by Atlanta's white business community, which historically had won all airport business. They protested that minority businesses were not capable of providing the level of services required and that it was unlawful to require minority participation. To the degree that was true, it was because these same businesses had colluded to exclude minorities at every opportunity.

Jackson was not to be dissuaded from his effort, and ultimately threatened to completely shut down the expansion effort unless and until minority businesses were located and brought to the table.

When the white establishment recognized Jackson's determination—and executive power to see it through—it set about finding ways to carry out his mandate without suffering itself. Among the solutions:

1. Contracts were broken into smaller segments so that a contractor would not be required to have multi-millions of dollars of insurance and capability to bid on the contracts.

2. Each request for bids/proposals would contain a requirement for a specified minimum minority participation in the project. (This provision was later overturned by court action in a Richmond, Virginia, case. The court said it *was* permissible to contain these provisions as a target.)

Jackson's determination resulted in hundreds of millions of dollars of construction and concession work being awarded to minority contractors and businesses for the first time.

During the 1950s, '60s and '70s, my high school and college friend Herman Russell had built a tremendous success in construction and construction management. He was always looking to grow his business interests, and minority set-asides put his company into overdrive. He landed airport construction contracts that opened doors for him across Atlanta and the state of Georgia.

One of the early non-construction operations that Herman became interested in was the food and beverage concessions at Hartsfield.

At the time, my law firm, Kutak Rock & Huie, was representing Host International, which was one of the world's largest airport concessionaires. Host was seeking the concessions contract at Hartsfield Airport, and it needed representation from a local law firm. It hired Kutak, and William Ide and I worked together with the client. In the course of daily business, I got to know its general counsel and CEO.

With the changes brought to the airport by Maynard Jackson, Host needed a local minority business partner to contend for the Hartsfield Airport business.

Bill Ide and I introduced Host to Herman, who formed Concessions International and partnered with Host International to submit a proposal to go after the major concessions at the Atlanta airport. They were one of three bidders and finished ... third.

But in the process, a solid relationship developed among Host, Herman and me. Their CEO and Herman, in particular, really hit it off, opening the door to another opportunity ... 2,175 miles away in California. Host's general counsel and I also hit it off.

Host was already the master concessionaire at Los Angeles International Airport (LAX), but it was under pressure from L.A.'s first African-American mayor, Tom Bradley, to sub-contract a portion of its LAX business to a minority contractor.

Re-enter Herman.

The problem was that Herman did not have the requisite food industry experience that the enterprise required—but I did.

I successfully owned and operated three Burger King stores in Atlanta that I had to give up when I became a full-time attorney at law. (I also had owned and operated—less successfully—a Chinese restaurant with my cousin James Brooks, who was a master chef. We called it "Oriental Kitchen." The problem was not that two African-Americans were running an Asian restaurant; my cousin did a great job of putting the menu together, offering what I still think was some of the best Chinese food in the city. It failed because it was designed by a master chef, as opposed to a businessman. We had the best eggrolls you've ever had in your life. But you couldn't sell them at the price it cost us to prepare them! After pouring all the money I cared to lose into it, we shut it down.)

Herman was aware of this and approached me with an offer to become a part owner in his new company, Concessions International.

When we got back together after my years in the Army, our friendship picked up right where we left off in college, but it also grew into this business relationship. We always felt that we would be good partners.

I saw the potential and was excited about going into business with this man who had not only been a close friend in high school, but was also my college roommate. When I started my military career, Herman and I talked about the possibility of one day going into the construction business together. I had studied building trades at Tuskegee and he was already in that business, having started with his father as a boy and building homes in high school. We agreed that when I got out of the Army, we would work together, expecting that I would be in the Army for three years and then get out. It didn't go that way, and I stayed with the service for 20 years. By then, our lives and dreams had changed.

I accepted and plunked down my share of the cost—$30,000—for 20 percent of the business.[20]

---

[20] Mary permitted me to mortgage our home to raise the $30,000 I needed to finance the business.

Los Angeles Mayor Tom Bradley, left, and Felker Ward Jr.

Our mutual friend Jesse Hill, chairman of Atlanta Life, matched my investment and joined us in the enterprise.

The first opportunity for CI was at Los Angeles Airport.

Host won a new contract at LAX requiring a minority contractor partner and—as might be expected—turned over the least business that it could, the restaurant and cocktail lounge in Terminal 2, LAX's international—and smallest—terminal at the time. But we were a startup, and

Host helped us get organized, taught us the ropes and got the enterprise off the ground. It was not a high-volume business, but it was profitable.

When LAX opened its new international facility in 1984 to coincide with Los Angeles hosting the Summer Olympics, Tom Bradley International Terminal, it was much larger and offered a variety of food concessions and cocktail lounges. Host International had its eye on that concession, but the LAX board—chaired by attorney Johnnie Cochran[21]—said, "No, Concessions International is now working for the airport at its international terminal. And since this is the new international terminal—replacing their existing service contract—they should continue."

This was a gigantic leap forward for Concessions International, which later went on to own and operate food and beverage concessions and gift and news stores in our hometown of Atlanta, as well as Cleveland, Chicago, Orlando, New Orleans, Hartford, Seattle-Tacoma, New York/JFK and Portland, Oregon.

Over the years, Concessions International grew in size and scale, and offered financial and management assistance to smaller, start-up minority companies across the United States, just as Host once gave us a leg up.

•••

The first deal was 60 percent Herman, 20 percent Jesse, and 20 percent Felker because Herman already had an agreement in place with Host. Ultimately, it was agreed that Jesse and I would purchase an additional interest in the enterprise to equalize our ownership at one-third interest apiece.

Herman had the most enviable balance sheet of the three of us, and at times that balance sheet was important, although Jesse and I invested in the enterprise the same amount as Herman did.

I became the chief operating officer of Concessions. The title didn't mean all that much, except that it was my responsibility to manage the day-to-day operations. My management experience came not only from owning Burger King stores but also from a military career dedicated to efficiency and organization; those factors combined to make me a natural as our operations officer.

We wound up being the largest minority-owned airport concessions company in America.

As we went about seeking new airport concessions contracts around the country, I was the one who would take our staff to visit new potential business sites.

None of us was ever full-time at Concessions. We never maintained

---

[21] Johnnie Cochran later became a national celebrity as O.J. Simpson's defense attorney when the former NFL star was accused of murdering his wife and a friend.

an office or a desk there.

Chasing new deals and figuring out how to structure our bids was always exciting to me. The cities made their airport decisions based on our experience and expertise in the field but, most important, they always chose the best bid for their tax coffers. How much could we bid and win, but still make money? You don't want to get the bid and then lose money, so the bids took a lot of work.

Jesse Hill had an equally important role in this enterprise. It seemed like he knew someone in every city in America. He was a master of networking decades before LinkedIn. How? For starters, Jesse raised a lot of money over the years for the Congressional Black Caucus. All the politicians knew him and respected him. The Atlanta Life Insurance Company, of which he was president, had offices in several cities around the country. That raised his profile nationwide.

The person representing Concessions International who located and solicited potential local disadvantaged business enterprises (DBE) partners was Jesse. He would identify those folks and Herman's daughter, Donata, and I cut deals with them. He was also the one who guided us through bureaucratic red tape everywhere Concessions International landed.

It started small, but as it grew, it became a high-revenue generator not only for me, but also for Herman, who simultaneously sustained a successful real estate development and management empire apart from Concessions.

In Cleveland, the local partner Jesse found for us was Carole Hoover, an African-American woman running the Greater Cleveland Growth Association, which was unusual. All the businessmen around her—and they were mostly men, few women—were almost all white. The position of influence that she had achieved was a real tribute to who she was and still is.

Jesse's role at Seattle-Tacoma International Airport was slightly different. The administration at SeaTac was not interested in having a new minority firm come on board, and when we approached them about the possibility of getting a concession contract there, they said, "We have a contract with Host and it has ten years to go. And at the end of that ten years, we'll entertain your interest in coming in."

We said, no, we wouldn't be interested in waiting a decade. We'd like to compete *now*.

We took our case directly to the airport authority, where Jesse had already made the acquaintance of a couple senior board members. Jesse convinced them to say to the airport administration, "We want you to bring in a minority firm, and we're not willing to wait ten years for it to happen."

As it turned out, a couple of years before we got involved at SeaTac, the airport had extended its lease with Host International. We used that as an argument: By extending their lease, you are not bound to one operator. You can bring in others, during which time it could and should have modified the ownership structure.

Jesse told us that one of the airport commissioners whose endorsement we needed was on a cruise. Jesse found a way, by helicopter perhaps, to get to that commissioner at sea, and get his endorsement for our deal. He told Herman and me that the weather was so bad, real bad, the boat was rocking all over the place. But he hung in there and got this commissioner's endorsement. That was a typical, legendary Jesse Hill maneuver.

Landing a contract at John F. Kennedy Airport in New York City was more classic Jesse Hill territory. He knew elected officials in New York, but he especially knew religious leaders from coast to coast who were well-known, respected and influential. Gaining their endorsement and having their support was always advantageous to the cause of minority-owned small businesses.

•••

Jesse taught me the art of grandfatherhood. He took it to an art form. If you didn't believe it, just let one of his grandchildren call him with some issue or problem. Jesse would give up everything else that he was doing and accommodate that child. He was unequivocal in his love of those children.

The second thing that mattered to me about Jesse Hill was that he was a one-of-a-kind friend.

If I could only have one friend in my life, who would it be? I have had magnificent friends in my life and benefited from all of the good things that flow from those relationships. But if I had to narrow it down to one person, the most complete would be Jesse Hill. (I think Herman would have said the same thing.) There was no such thing as a casual relationship with Jesse Hill.

But if you wanted something done, give it to Jesse Hill and it always got done.

It was not unusual for Jesse to call me at 5 in the morning, and the first words out of his mouth would be, "Did I call too early? You want me to call you back?"

My answer would be, "No, you've already awakened me now, there's no point in talking about calling me back and doing it again!"

On New Year's Day, he'd be the first person to wish you a Happy New Year.

Another time, I was with Jesse and he had on a pair of new shoes that I admired. I said, "Jesse, those are some nice-looking shoes you've got there." The next day FedEx knocked at my door with two pairs of those shoes—in two different sizes. He didn't know which would fit me, so he sent me two pairs.

He was a friend among friends. If you were his friend, by God, you were his friend, and he was your friend.

Herman met him first, soon after Jesse came to Atlanta. I was in the Army and had not yet gotten situated back home. Jesse was the first African-American president of the Atlanta Chamber of Commerce; in fact, he was the first African-American elected president of any chamber in a major U.S. city. He was the first African-American on the board of Delta Air Lines. He was first on the board of Knight Ridder, which owned the *Miami Herald, Philadelphia Inquirer, San Jose Mercury News* and many other major newspapers. When African-American businessmen in Atlanta needed financing, Jesse was the one who opened the door for them at Citizens & Southern Bank (C&S).

Jesse was originally from St. Louis, Missouri, and attended Lincoln University. He earned a post-graduate degree from the University of Michigan. He came to Atlanta, he often said, with nothing more than a knapsack on his back.

The founder and chairman of Atlanta Life Insurance Company, Mr. Norris Herndon, took an early liking to Jesse and brought him on as an actuary. He identified Jesse as the person whom he eventually wanted to lead his company and he groomed him for years to fill that role.

In addition to our business together, Herman, Jesse and I—and our wives—frequently socialized together. We took trips together to Jamaica, Florida and elsewhere.

•••

As for Herman, he was an entrepreneur at heart—all the way back to when we were teenagers. He had a joint on Auburn Avenue where he flipped hamburgers. It was his own restaurant at a time when most of us would be out either hunting or fishing or playing sports or something. But Herman was working—and earning.

Herman was always industrious. The thing that really worked to his benefit was that, unlike most small-business people, Herman didn't spend all his money. He saved a good bit. Minority small-business opportunities came to be in vogue as more and more cities—and the federal government—put in place hard and fast requirements for minority business participation in the largesse of governmental expenditures and opportunities. Herman was well-situated to make the most of opportunities. He was able to get construction bonding, which can be a severe limitation on otherwise qualified minority small-business contractors. They can't take big multi-million-dollar construction jobs because they can't get bonding at that level. Herman was one of the best contractors in the city of Atlanta—in fact, he was one of the biggest in the entire country. That was the spring-board for him that brought about much of his success. He prepared for it, and he never wasted his money. He was always tight with a buck; he'd be the first to admit it. But it paid dividends at the end of the day.[22]

•••

One of Herman's requirements to be in business with him was that you had to carry your share of the financial load. That was certainly the case with Concessions International; he didn't take Jesse or me on as part-ners because we were friends. In that regard, he could be tough and un-yielding. He would not finance someone else's ownership share. His en-trepreneurial bent went back to his youth. And it matured by the time he was a grown man.

I don't think Herman ever changed any more than simply getting older. He was always fun loving, for example, and that never changed. (As adults, whenever Herman and I enjoyed a successful commercial venture or personal achievement, we always said to each other, "This is a long way from 111!"—referring to our college street address.)

---

[22] At the height of social unrest in many American cities in the 1960s, civic and business communities in Atlanta formed a coalition of white and black business leaders to help Atlanta get ahead of the problem of, hopefully, avoiding the riot experiences in the City. (Atlanta had experienced a taste of this unrest a few years prior.)

The coalition came to be known as the Action Forum. I joined the group upon my retirement from active-duty military. The idea took wing under the leadership of Mills Lane and William Alexander. The group was initially comprised of six black and six white members. Over the years, the organization grew in size, but generally remained of equal black and white member balance.

In order for the coalition to be effective, we agreed upon several tenets. First, our discussions were off the record and were generally no-holds-barred. It was a forum in which various opinions could be free of attack with the assurance that they were being kept within the bosom of the body itself. The second was that elected individuals were not members. From this initiative, quite a few of the members, after getting to know each other, became lifelong friends.

The Action Forum, in its regular form, does not exist today. It might be assumed that the reason for its demise was that its members concluded that there was no longer a need for the organization. Frankly, I think this was unfortunate, because there are still a myriad of issues in our city that could effectively be dealt with by an organization like the Action Forum.

I handled day-to-day relationships with vendors, our employees and with airport managers. The three us were the board of Concessions International, and we made decisions together as we went along.

Concessions International was never the primary job of any one of the three of us. We provided whatever attention and management it needed at any given time and never put on paper specific responsibilities for any of us. We applied and combined our individual strengths to make the enterprise work. Each of us had something to contribute to the success of the enterprise, and that's what we brought to the table.

•••

Being business partners in Concessions International took a toll on our personal relationships. The three of us became more business partners first and friends second. In terms of our social lives, we interacted some, but as we grew older we all had our own groups of friends, our own lives, our own children.

I lived in southwest Atlanta; Jesse lived closer in to the city; and Herman lived in another area, so we were not neighbors.

Not to say that we didn't do some things together; over the years, we always took our wives out together for dinner on Valentine's Day. That was a tradition with us before Herman's first wife, Otelia, passed away in 2006 and it continued when he met and married Sylvia a few years later.

Our lives took directions of their own because of the differences in our professions. I pursued a legal career and built friendships around it. Many of my friends were fellow lawyers, judges and people involved in the legal system. Jesse was CEO of Atlanta Life, and that took him in the direction of insurance. Herman was a contractor, developer and investor not just in Atlanta but throughout the South. The hanging out together that we did in college just didn't fit our lifestyle as adults.

In 1999, I was ready to sell my interest in the business because of a couple of things. I saw the future in what we were doing as cloudy. We were principally in the restaurant business at airports, but the airports were dramatically changing their relationships with their lessees. For one thing, they wanted name brands in airports. A few years earlier, you never saw a Chick-fil-A, Burger King, Wendy's or a McDonald's in an airport. We had our own labels, our own franchises, and we were not spending money paying franchise fees. Second, the airports came up with a concept they called "street pricing." That meant if you paid a buck fifty for a Big Mac in downtown Atlanta, then we couldn't charge but a buck fifty for a Big Mac in the Atlanta airport. Great for consumers, but our rent structure was totally different from the off-airport franchisees and profits shrunk. Third, the airports demanded profit sharing. We ran our business and paid our expenses. What we made over and above those expenses was our profit. With the introduction of profit sharing in contracts, the airports wanted half of our profit, too! The fourth change was the end of our exclusivity. If we were in a certain terminal and we had the restaurant there, it was ours—the airport couldn't bring anybody else in. Most airports don't do exclusives anymore, so we might look up one day and find a restaurant just a few feet away competing with us and cannibalizing our business.

When I saw all of that, it became clear that the future of Concessions International's business was not as bright as it had been when we started. I felt that it was a good time to cash out.

The three of us being partners could be stressful at times, but all in all, we had a good working partnership. Our roles shifted a little bit at times, but it was always done with a focus on what was best for the company. For example, when we'd go after a new concession opportunity, most of the time we engaged a local partner. There was always a question of how and what should determine their share.

Herman, on the other hand, was not interested in selling. His daughter, Donata, was working for us and had risen through the ranks to become an excellent, incisive executive and natural leader. Herman was interested in passing the company along to her. That made a lot of sense to us.

"It was interesting working with H.J., Jesse Hill and Felker Ward," Donata said in 2016, "because they were three men with strong personalities who were individually accomplished and very demanding. Each one had his own unique things that they were looking for, which required me to always be thinking about not just one perspective, but all three of theirs plus my own. The employees used to call them 'The Three Musketeers.'

"Mr. Ward was the negotiator of the group. He was the one who was always interested in the details, the one who would negotiate contract terms, and the one to push us to consider the effects of requirements, leases and contract terms. He was the one who usually dealt with the airports, our landlords. He knew the people who were part of the airport administration, whereas H.J. was more concerned with the day-to-day operations of the facilities. Mr. Hill was more business development on the front end, finding out who the decision-makers were, coming up with a strategy for us to grow and win locations. They made for an interesting trio together.

"I worked with all three of them. But Mr. Ward was the one I usually called with operations questions and he gave me more assignments than anybody else, including my father. He was the one who always had something for me to do.

"There's this crazy story about the three of them about to miss a plane because they were late leaving a meeting. Mr. Hill flagged down a Federal Express truck, and they all rode in the back of this truck to the airport.

"Mrs. Ward was always so sweet. They really had contrasting

personalities. Mr. Ward, when he was younger, honestly, he was stern. He never let you get really close to him. I always knew him from more of a business standpoint. Mrs. Ward was the total opposite. She was just sweet Mary. I have fond memories of just spending time with her, and her being so engaging and accommodating and nice.

"Their personalities were starkly different. You didn't piss him off, or you were not his friend for a long time. But I've seen him mellow over the years. To me, he's a different person now.

"Mr. Ward was not an easy person to work with for anybody. What I appreciated about him was that even though he was tough, he did pull out the best in you. He would cause you to double-check and dot the i's and cross the t's whenever you were preparing something for him. I guess it really gets back to that military training. And then he was a lawyer and a negotiator, so you could never really argue with him. It was hard to present another opinion to him. That's why I think we all learned to possibly go to H.J. or Mr. Hill with concerns and let them handle that with Mr. Ward.

"The three of them could be in a closed-door meeting, and you could hear every word they were saying through the walls, because they were all trying to get their point across.

"I learned more about reading contracts and understanding leases from working with Mr. Ward, because I took business law in college. Sometimes young lawyers just want to brush over stuff. Working for Mr. Ward caused me to look much broader at what we're trying to do and thinking through what would certain clauses mean long-term if A, B or C happened. Based on different scenarios, what would this mean? He wasn't afraid to ask for things that may not have seemed possible, and many times would get those added or some variation of those added. I learned quite a bit when it came to negotiating contract administration from him."

We had in our partnership agreement a first right of refusal, which said that if anyone wants to buy one of us out, the other partner has a right to match that price and purchase that partner's interest. That's what Herman wanted to do, and he offered Jesse and me the equivalent of what Host proposed to pay, so it worked out just fine.

Jesse and I sold our interest in Concessions International outright to Herman. There were other concessions businesses—aside from Concessions International—in which the three of us were joint investors and we maintained our individual interest in those, including a dozen gift shops in the St. Louis airport. We were also partners and investors in a duty-free operation at JFK with a company called Duty Free Americas.

IV. FATHER, GRANDFATHER, HUNTER, FISHERMAN

26. CHURCH LIFE

Church has always held an important place in my life. It is not only a place for religious worship, but it has also been a primary place for social interaction since I was a little boy.

My family attended church every Sunday for Bible School followed immediately by noon-day worship. I was reared in what was called the Holiness faith, a form of worship that is evangelical in nature. In our worship service, we lived out the notion of "make a joyful noise unto the Lord." We sang songs, accompanied by a bass drum, tambourines, cymbals and, on many occasions, piano and guitar. We generally did not have songbooks, but we learned the songs by heart. My favorite contribution was beating the drums. My mother, however, was forever reminding me that I was not keeping good time!

It was also not unusual for some members of the congregation to joyfully clap their hands to the music, while other parishioners rose to their feet to dance to the music and "get happy."

Services at our church were frequented by people from a wide area, who joined us to hear and enjoy the sounds of our devotion. A typical service involved a singing session led by one of the men of the church, followed by a "testimony" service. This was the time when members could "testify" as to how good God had been to them during the past week. By this time, we were already 90 self-guided minutes into the week's service. The pastor would then rise and take charge.

There was no seminary affiliated with our church and, for the most part, our pastors and other leaders were not seminary-trained. They were generally selected as "shepherds" because first, they could read and help interpret the Scriptures, and second, they were men who were upright

Me, with Mom and Dad.

leaders in the community. They honed their preaching skills through practice. Our congregations did not attract enough money to pay a pastor full-time, and therefore, this was part-time work. They all had other regular day jobs. It was also not unusual for a pastor to be the shepherd of more than one church. He would visit one church on a given Sunday, and a different church the next.

I have referred to the pastors in the masculine gender. That is because we did not have female pastors. Women were called "mothers" of the church, and they taught Sunday School and other lessons, but they did not occupy the role as pastors. Promising young men who were members of the church were identified early on, and permitted to take charge of leadership aspects within the services. It was from this cadre of young men that future pastors were ultimately chosen. Pastors who grew their preaching skills and leadership abilities were identified and selected as presiding elders, a role in which there were several pastors assigned to them. These leaders had authority to appoint pastors from the pool of upcoming preachers and, bishops were selected from the pool of elders.

The women were not completely left out. The leading sisters—the mothers of the parish—had authority over certain administrative and ecclesiastical functions. The good ones were also called up to teach, but not to preach. The mothers wore robes, and in my opinion, were the true backbone of the church. As I reflect on the churches in which I grew up, it was the mothers more than the pastors whom I remember the most. With the exception of my father, of course, who was a pastor.

Dad rose to the position of presiding elder before he eventually retired from active pastoring. Retiring, mind you, did not mean with pay. There was no money for retirement pay for our retiring ministers.

I enjoyed attending my dad's churches with him on Sundays, even when my mother and brother did not go. They generally had Sunday dinner in honor of the pastor, and oh, boy, did the congregation ever pass out a tremendous amount of food!—usually several meat dishes, salads, cooked vegetables, desserts, you name it. I was a teenager and consumed tons of food without gaining a pound.

There was a strong belief among us that men and women should marry within the denomination. That is, to a member of the same faith. My mother and father adhered to that belief. My mother was a member of the Holiness faith, and a few years after she died, when my father decided to remarry, it was to another member of the church.

Our church labored under the belief that water baptism was not necessary. They cited Scriptures to support this belief. I later became convinced that this was a misreading of the Scriptures, and I, personally, was baptized twice in the Episcopal Church. The reason was that I did not remember my first baptism, although my wife reminded me that I had been baptized at the end of my confirmation in the Episcopal Church. Since I did not remember that part of it, I decided that being baptized twice was much safer than not being baptized at all!

As I moved around the world on military assignments, I always found a church, and it did not matter what denomination. Military religious services were largely ecumenical.

When I was a young lieutenant and a platoon leader, on Sunday mornings I went to the barracks where my platoon was housed, and I invited others to join me for church. This was not a requirement; some joined me, others did not. (I doubt that we could get away with that practice in the military today.)

Later when I was a company commander in Aschaffenburg, Germany, my home was only a few blocks from my headquarters. Consequently, I was able to go home for lunch on most days. In doing so, I stopped at the chapel daily and enjoyed a few moments of quiet meditation. Occasionally, the chaplain would see me there and join me, kneeling beside me without a word spoken.

Later, when I was stationed in Vietnam during the heat of the war, on most Sundays I took time from combat to worship. We worked, of course, seven days a week, but pretty soon everyone around me, including superior officers, respected this habit of mine and honored my private time. In fact, quite a few of them joined me for chapel service on Sunday mornings. Services were held in our headquarters building and organized by our post chaplain.

•••

When our children were young, Mary and I taught them the importance of Christian teaching and worship. We found the most complete and compatible teaching for them to be in the Episcopal Church. We were confirmed in St. Luke's Episcopal Church in Atlanta by the Rev. Dan Matthews.

The attraction of St. Luke's was that it had the most manifest way of living out our religious beliefs. This was demonstrated by a daily program feeding the homeless, a clothing bank and a jobs program. For some years, Mary administered a jobs program under the guidance of the Rev. Reynell Parkins, and I served on the vestry for several years.

We are now members of St. Paul's Episcopal Church in Atlanta. When we joined St. Paul's, the rector was the Right Rev. Robert Wright. In October 2012, we lost Rector Wright when the diocese elected him as its first black bishop—and 10th overall—making him the third elected bishop of Atlanta and the first African-American to ever hold this esteemed office.

27. THE HUNTER

Hunting, I'm convinced, is part of my DNA.

I started hunting when I was a kid. My dad was a hunter of small game—rabbit, squirrels, raccoons, possum. At that time in Georgia or Alabama, we didn't have access to wild turkeys or deer, so we hunted small game. When my younger brother, Solomon, got old enough to hunt, it was the three of us and two of my dad's brothers on the hunt every Saturday in the winter. We always had a good coon dog and a good possum dog and a good rabbit dog and a good squirrel dog. They were the key to enjoyable hunting.

One of my dad's brothers, Samuel, had 13 children, many of them boys. We each had to have boots for hunting. And when you're going on an all-day hunt, you've got to have food and potable water. We took food that you could easily transport in a sack on our backs—sardines, cheese, crackers and potted meat. We didn't have canteens like we do now, so we drank the water that we encountered while hunting. We knew how to decide what water to drink and what water we couldn't drink: a running stream that went over rocks and sand, that water was okay to drink. Still water was contaminated; we didn't drink that. Water never made us sick, so apparently we were doing it the right way.

There were occasions when we would encounter a stream that was maybe a foot or so deep, and I remember when I was very young that my dad used to put me on his back and carry me across those streams. If my brother was with us, my Uncle Samuel took him across. Their main goal was to help us keep our boots dry for walking all day.

The men always had a lot of fun together on the hunt; we always had something to laugh about.

In those days, none of us had much money so we didn't waste shotgun

Felker Ward Jr.

shells or anything else. We would kid my uncle and say he shot his weapons three times and wound up with four rabbits! We didn't have coyotes back in those days in Georgia, so rabbits were plentiful. It was not unusual to bed a rabbit. That meant you might walk by him and the rabbit did not run. He didn't realize that we saw him, so he stayed put. My dad and uncle were not just sportsmen; they were also meat hunters, so they would kill a bedded rabbit. My uncle would hit them upside the head with his shotgun. That's how he caught a rabbit without using a shell. He was noted for his ability to bed rabbits more than any of the other hunters we knew.

One of the most wonderful memories I have is when we went to Tuskegee, and Dad acquired a couple of good squirrel dogs. We spent as many Saturday afternoons as we could in the wintertime hunting squirrels with our dogs. It was a good time together. When we returned in the afternoon, my mother cooked the game. She knew how to prepare it all so it was very, very tasty.

When I was 10 years old, my dad would let me go along with him on a small-game hunt with no gun, just to be out there with him. I enjoyed that. One November, I was walking behind my dad and I spotted a rabbit that he had walked right past and didn't see. I got his attention and he shot the rabbit. That same year, I got my first gun for Christmas. Dad felt I was finally old enough to handle a gun safely. So my Christmas present was a combination shotgun and rifle. It was a .22 rifle and a .410 shotgun, an all-in-one weapon. I kept that weapon—and hunted with it—into adulthood.

Dad always had three or four friends we hunted with, but for a long time, I was the only kid in the group.

One of our traditions was that my dad and brother Solomon and I, along with my dad's brothers, always went hunting on Thanksgiving Day.

I distinctly remember buying my first deer rifle, a Weatherby .270 caliber, in 1966. My first deer hunt was with a fellow pilot at Fort Meade, Maryland, by the name of John Downey.

My love for hunting continues to this day; it is a sport in which I engage at every opportunity. I have hunted in many places in the United States, as well as in Argentina, Germany, Zimbabwe, Namibia and Canada.

It is my practice that I only hunt game that we will consume. The only single exception is a black bear I killed in Alaska.

You have to look at what I do for a hobby to find my friends. And I love to hunt. My hunting friends include Dr. Bill McClatchey, Dave Cole, Herschel Jones, Bob Jones, Willie Johnson, Georgia Supreme Court Justice Robert Benham, Dr. Charles Wilmer, Roy Barnes, Ray Barnes and

Richard Allen. We don't socialize that much together, but when hunting season is near, we stay in close touch.

I graduated to large-game hunting in a couple of different countries in Africa more than 25 years ago thanks to McClatchey, my friend and my physician until he retired from practicing in 2016. We met serving on a board together and I found out that he was a fellow hunter.

McClatchey and I hunted all over the world for more than 25 years. One of our hunts was for moose in Canada. I killed a 700-pound animal in the middle of nowhere. How could I get him out? How could I get him back home to prepare the meat? The outfitters used packhorses. We had to butcher the animal right there on the ground, in the field or in the woods. There was no way to pick him up. It was a real field operation.

McClatchey's daughter has gone on hunting trips with us, but she didn't hunt. She went along for the joy of being with us in a foreign country. Occasionally one of her girlfriends would come along to keep her company. It's not a sport where we had women along very often.

In Colorado, we hunt for elk at a ranch owned by Ray Barnes. Ray is the brother of Roy Barnes, the former governor of Georgia. Roy will often join our hunt.

When elk hunting in Colorado, there are trails and roads throughout the ranch. We know our way around, and we rent a four-wheel vehicle that can get us into the wilderness and get our game out. Ray has an old Ford truck with a winch on the back. We call it the "Elkmobile." It's used to drag the elk, once it's killed, out of the woods and transport it to Craig, Colorado, the little town there where they have processing operations to get the meat ready for the skillet.

You can't just up one day and say, "I'm going elk hunting." It takes a lot of preparation and it's not cheap.

Ray has several thousand acres of real estate and ranches in Colorado. He and my brother Solomon knew each other first, which was how I got to know the Barnes family.

In the quieter moments of a hunt, we talk about some of the ills of the world and exchange ideas on these trips, but I have a philosophy that, in these settings, there are three things I generally don't spend much time talking about: race, religion and politics. Why? Because I find you don't change anybody's view of it, and generally it winds up with everybody on a different side of the fence. Nothing is accomplished by talking about these three subjects on a hunting trip. We talk about some controversial topics but, generally, not pure politics. I'm not all that loyal to a single party. My view depends upon what I think of the particular candidate's philosophy. I'm more hung up on what you stand for. What's the nature of the candidate's character? That's the way I pick for whom I will vote.

Instead, we talk about family; we talk about sports. Two of my fellow hunters are well-known physicians, so sometimes we'll talk about health-care issues. I find it interesting to hear their perspective.

It is a joy to sit over a martini and listen to Roy Barnes tell stories about things that happened in the state of Georgia during his years in office.

I partner with a group of other hunters who lease quail-hunting rights on a large plantation in South Carolina—Turkey Hill. It is a nice hunting experience. We are quartered in the "big house," a beautiful home owned by the Milbank Family.

In early fall, they put out quail in several courses. By the time we hunt these birds, they are truly wild birds. The guides ride on horseback and the hunters ride in a wagon operated by "Bubba."

I invite three fellow hunters at a time. Strict safety rules are observed and followed.

The bird dogs used on this plantation are pointers and retrievers.

Quail hunting at Turkey Hill is somewhat expensive. Everyone has their own private bedroom, and we have cooks and servants who prepare food and serve us three meals a day. It's a first-class operation. I sometimes lament the fact that of all my African-American friends, 90 percent of them don't hunt. Some of them play golf. But I don't golf anymore, mainly because I don't have time.

You become a member of one of these hunting groups by invitation only. The only way you can get into the group is for somebody to die or go broke and not pay the atrocious fees it takes to manage this kind of operation.

As a kid, I would not have been able to afford the kind of hunting that I do now. Just think of an airline fare to Africa and back; the airfare alone might cost that much. If we're hunting big game in Africa, the outfitter fee will include hunting, a guide, food and lodging. In some places, such as Africa, there's an extra fee for every animal you kill.

In South Dakota, we hunt pheasant. We stay in a real nice hotel where the cocktail lounge opens at our discretion. And that one is not all that expensive, including food, lodging, hunting and the dressing of the birds.

For the South Dakota pheasant hunt, there is an outfitter that contracts with local farmers to grow crops that will be attractive to pheasants. That's how we have such good luck there. Some people, naturally, are a better shot than others. As a sidebar, I will reveal to you, dear reader, that there is only one person in the group my age; actually, he's a couple of years older than I am. But I get special treatment. On part of the hunt that's called a "drive," when we're pushing through a big field to flush out the birds, I don't have to do that. I get on the end down there, where the birds are going to come out on the other end. It's where I let my age give me a little bit of advantage.

The deer hunts are on property that I own in Pike County, Georgia. We stay in fully equipped campers. The hunter in our group who enjoyed doing the cooking for us died, so now we go out to a restaurant for our meals. But we still sit around a campfire at night and talk. We solve the world's biggest problems right there!

I never got lectures about safety from Dad or his friends; I learned by watching them.

I saw that they always unloaded their guns when they got to the car. They never put a loaded shotgun in the car. They unloaded their guns, so I unload mine. And you have to always keep track of where your fellow hunters are. Sometimes you're in tall grass, tall weeds or in brush, and you can't see everybody. In order to avoid an accident, it's important that each hunter knows where all the other hunters are. That's something I learned by instinct and by watching experienced hunters.

I do get safety lectures now. The outfitters we hunt with all give safety lectures, as well they should. Some people have a lot of experience hunting, and some have little or no experience. The outfitters have to talk to everyone about the do's and don'ts of hunting. To me, however, it's sort of like a rabbit dog. How do you train a rabbit dog? Well, you take it out in the woods and let it run rabbits. Some people in Georgia and Alabama will fence in maybe 8 or 10 acres and put rabbits in there. You train rabbit dogs by turning them loose. Their natural instinct is to run rabbits and to do it by scent, as opposed to by sight. It's a natural development that doesn't take any instructions. Put the dogs out with rabbits and leave them a couple of weeks. Then take the dogs hunting and they'll run rabbits for you.

Generally speaking, I am a late riser, but I make an exception for hunting. I don't get up early just for the fun of it. But if I've got something to do like hunting, by God I'll get up whatever time I need to. We get up at 4:30 in the morning to hunt. So by the time 8 p.m. comes, we're ready for bed.

•••

My children are less interested in hunting than I am. My youngest, Wes, is a good hunter and a sharpshooter. He doesn't have much time to devote to sports and his first choice is golf. The only time he will hunt is when it's not good golfing weather.

The difference between my growing up and my kids' is that they had a myriad of things that they could do: football, baseball, soccer, swimming. They were always engaged in a lot of things. My brother Solomon and I didn't have access to any of that when we were growing up. We didn't have access to a swimming pool. We didn't have Little League-type sports that we could engage in. Hunting and fishing, if you were lucky enough to have a dad who enjoyed doing those things, was a good and special thing.

My middle son, Jay, hunted with me a few times, but he wore glasses most of his life and I always suspected that his sight limitations had some effect on his enjoyment of the sport.

Mary never objected to me introducing the kids to hunting; as I've said, she's a good hunter's wife. She was never interested in hunting with me but she learned how to prepare the game. She doesn't eat it herself but, like my mom, she learned how to prepare it properly, so that it's tasty. I never heard her express any concerns about them hunting with me.

One of the things that Mary and I used to do from time to time—and I'm sure it's totally illegal now and maybe it was then—was go out on a country road at night with a .22 rifle. Mary would be behind the wheel and I shot rabbits as they ran across the road. They would stop and we turned the car light on them. But in general, she wanted no part of the game until it came time to cook it. I do have a few friends whose wives hunt, but most of them don't.

•••

If it weren't for hunters, there would be a serious problem with the overrun of wild animals—especially deer. The best friend of the deer population in Georgia and Alabama happens to be the hunters, who help keep the population down. Alabama created extremely restrictive hunting laws a few years ago and the herd outgrew the state's carrying capacity. They incurred bluetongue disease, which made the deer sickly and inedible. It was a terrible situation. Georgia and Alabama realized they were over-managing the herd and got it back on track.

•••

Mary encourages my hunting. I couldn't have found a better person for understanding what's good to keep her husband happy.

Of course, I go out of my way to keep her happy, too. We do a lot of things together. We've been blessed and fortunate in a financial sense, so we're able to do most anything we want to do.

She is a bridge player. As long as she gets a chance to get in a good game of bridge at least once a week—sometimes twice a week—she's good to go.

We have a house on Lake Oconee where we like to escape for boating, fishing and water sports.

Mary and I have traveled extensively; we've had a good, lively life

I caught the large fish in the photos above near Islamorada, Florida.

together. The one thing I've learned is, if I keep her happy, I can go off and do my hunting. McClatchey and I are sensitive to our wives in this regard. Our wives go along with our desire to hunt regularly, so we don't abuse it. Because that's a recipe for getting in trouble. My advice: make sure that you prioritize what your partner wants to do, as well as what you want to do.

•••

Fishing is a part of my life, also.

My dad and mom and Solomon and I fished with cane poles and earthworms that we dug up in the yard. Or we used crickets. My mother and dad both loved to fish, as did my mother's mother, until she died at 90.

There are all sorts of fishing that we do.

We have a lake in our back yard, and we fish there for bass, bream, catfish and crappie. But Mary and I also love deep-sea fishing in Florida, from Destin in the Panhandle south to Marco Island. We also fish with friends for halibut and salmon in Seward, Valdez or Homer, Alaska.

It's said that 90 percent of the weight of our bodies is water. Water is soothing to me, and I think to most people. Being out on the water relaxes us. It's quiet and we bait a hook, throw it overboard, and wait for a fish to decide to test that morsel that we've thrown for him. And you hook him! Then he runs and bends the pole and so forth, and it's just a big thrill.

When we go, we charter a private boat of our own. It's a thrill being on the water and being out and being with people you enjoy being with. It's a lot of fun. I don't like to fish on boats that have 30 or 40 people on there.

There is a technique to catching fish that you learn from doing it. For example, if you're trawling, well, there's no technique to that. It's just the captain guiding the boat and you're trawling. But if you've got an anchor out and you're fishing in a spot, some people will catch more fish than others because they know how to do it. For example, say you're seeking grouper or red snapper. You do that by fishing along the bottom. It's important to know exactly how deep to go, whether to go all the way to the bottom, or a foot off the bottom, or whatever. Yes, there's a lot of luck in it. But there's also some technique required in successful fishing.

P.S. If you were to ask Mary, she would tell you *she's* the best fisherman in the family, which might be true.

28. CASA: A VIEW FROM THE TOP

The secretary of the Army has a program that none of the other service secretaries have.

CASA—Civilian Aide to the Secretary of the Army—is a program wherein the secretary identifies appropriate residents in each state and appoints them as civilian aides. The program provides a means of connectivity between the secretary and his office and private citizens. These CASAs, as they're called, are expected to articulate the Army's status and mission to the general public.

The other side of it, though, is to bring messages back to the secretary regarding ways the Army can improve communication with the outside world and to improve the view that citizens have of military service.

In 1990, I received a call from Brig. Gen. Donald Scott, who at the time was chief of staff of 1st Army at Forest Park. He wanted to know if I would be interested in being nominated as a civilian aide to the Secretary of the Army for the state of Georgia. Bernard "Bernie" Abrams was stepping down and thereby leaving the slot open. Scott encouraged me to offer my name for consideration for the CASA slot.

Gen. Scott was an officer with an outstanding military record who began his career as a ROTC graduate of Lincoln University in Missouri. He was once a professor of military science and tactics at Tuskegee University, my alma mater. Mary and I later became acquainted not only with Don but also with his wife, Betty. We enjoyed many good times together.

Before I could give an answer, that inquiry was followed by one from Abrams himself.

Both gentlemen made the same pitch. One, it would be an enjoyable and singular honor if I participated, and second, it would give me an opportunity to see the Army from a totally different point of view.

I had already seen the Army from the bottom up, as a young cadet in the ROTC, and ultimately, a second lieutenant in the Army, and finally as a lieutenant colonel. The CASA carries the protocol of three-star general and offers an opportunity to see the Army from the top down.

As someone who greatly valued his 20 years of training and service, I agreed to pursue the nomination alongside several others. I ultimately won the support of U.S. Sen. Sam Nunn, chairman of the Senate Armed Services Committee; Georgia Gov. George Busbee; and Bernie Abrams, the outgoing Georgia CASA. With the exception of Capt. Ben Fowler—my former supervisor at Fort Benning—each man sent a strong letter of support on my behalf.

One of the thrilling parts of being selected was that the installment ceremony would take place at Fort Benning, Georgia, the place where my military career started, and where I met my wife, Mary.

When I went into the program, most states had one CASA. New York and Texas, because of their size, each had two. Since then, however, Georgia has had two CASAs; other states may have more.

The secretary convenes a meeting of the CASAs once or twice a year, during which we are invited to spend three days getting briefed by the secretary and the Pentagon Army staff.

I was appointed by Michael P.W. Stone, the secretary of the Army under President George H.W. Bush. I served as a CASA for a number of years and then was granted emeritus status.

Active CASAs are expected to report quarterly on their activities to the secretary. Those reports are combined and published in a document shared with the other CASAs.

In 1990, during Desert Storm, I made quite a few speeches about the military to various Georgia chambers of commerce and other civic organizations.

I encouraged companies that were losing employees to the war effort to either hold their positions open or re-hire them when they come back out as veterans.

Nationally, CASAs encouraged companies to develop job programs for disabled veterans and jobs that did not require physical exertion for wounded warriors.

As a keynote speaker for the 1st Army and 3rd Army stationed in Georgia, as well as military academies and ROTC graduation classes, I talked to parents about what military life was all about and where we were as a military. My view was—and is—that the Army is one of the best finishing schools in America. I talked about the attributes that come forward in our soldiers in terms of reliability, trustworthiness and mutual support for one another, the kinds of things that make a unit cohesive and effective. These characteristics stand us well in the future, as we go through life. We have an all-volunteer Army, so it has to be attractive enough for volunteers to want to join.

•••

The military's approach to African-Americans had to evolve with the times, as it did with women. More recently, gay members of the service were scrutinized. For years, the policy was called "Don't ask, don't tell." It was a step forward but highly criticized in a lot of circles. The Army retired that policy in favor of normalizing the concept of LGBT members serving side by side. Once more, the military was ahead of much of society in terms of acceptance.

I noticed at some point that more and more of the places I would go as a CASA and CASA emeritus had a growing number of female senior officers. There had always been argument about whether women could perform physically—arguments once made about blacks by whites who did not want to see racial integration in the military. Their claims were false, then, totally false, and they rang false with each progressive group upon which they were applied. Able-bodied is able-bodied in today's Army; the soul of a patriot is still a patriot, whether white or black, male or female, straight, gay or transgender. I respect anyone who volunteers to put on the uniform of our country and vows to protect us from all threats.

We had our first female four-star general, finally, appointed in mid-2016. Women are flying fighter jets just as precisely as men. President Barack Obama's secretary of the Army, Eric Fanning, was openly gay, a remarkable development in the history of the American military. I would argue that he performed as well or better than any of his straight predecessors. He had no choice but to be better.

Having been on the receiving end of those who fought against my consideration as a black pilot half a century ago for no reason other than the color of my skin, I was a much more outspoken advocate of women and LGBT folks. That's the way life is. You and your thinking are the result of the totality of your personal experiences. I was faced with some genuine doubt about my ability simply because I was African-American. What I found myself facing was the need to be not just as good as a white man in my role, but better. I had to be better than my white male counterparts to be treated equally.

Today's "punching bag" might have been Muslims serving in the U.S. military, but when the 2016 election brought forward the story of Army Capt. Humayun Khan, who died while serving in Iraq in 2004, the public made it clear that a Muslim-American soldier killed in the protection of his unit and his country was every bit as American as anyone else.

•••

I met Army Gen. Larry Ellis when he was transitioning from the Pentagon to become the Forces Command Commander at Fort McPherson. He had just been promoted to four-star general and was reassigned from Washington in November 2001.

At the time Larry was promoted to four-star, he was just the fourth African-American four-star in the history of the U.S. Army.

The first was Roscoe Robinson Jr., a West Point graduate. The second was Colin Powell. The third was Johnnie E. Wilson. And the fourth, a year and a half later, was Larry. That was it for the first 230 years of U.S. Army history; since then, there have been several more.

I was the CASA in Georgia as Larry and his family transitioned to Fort McPherson and had the pleasure of helping introduce them to the community. I reached out to him as someone new to the community and wanted to make sure he met the right people and was greeted properly. The furthest he had ever been south in the United States for any length of time was Maryland; for him, Atlanta might as well have been Mars!

Sometime soon after that, Mary and I were delighted to host a dinner for Larry and his wife Jean in our home.

Larry was the G3 of the Army, which meant he was the chief of plans and operations for all the conventional Army forces in the United States—everything but training and special operations. He was also, after Colin Powell, the second minority to take this command. Colin was only in our city for about six months, and I wanted to make sure that Larry became involved in the community.

"He just grabbed me," Larry said. "And I appreciated it."

I had become one of the longest-serving of the national CASAs.

"Felker wanted to make sure that I, with the responsibility for all of the United States, took care of his state of Georgia."

The Force Com Commander had always been automatically welcomed as a member of the downtown Rotary Club. I was in my second year as president, which made it an added honor for Larry to join at that time.

"That was a monumental thing," Larry said. "You've got to put this in the perspective of race relations in Atlanta. It's real whether you like it or not. They wanted to elect an African-American because they'd never had one. Felker was the first individual to do that and that carried enormous weight."

As alien as Atlanta felt to Larry and his wife when they arrived in our city, it quickly grew on them because this is where they later retired when Larry stepped away from the service.

Gov. Roy Barnes had just won the 2001 election and Larry arrived in town the following week. Three months later, the four-star general received a call from the new governor, asking him to a meeting.

"General," Barnes said, "I need your help."

"Governor?"

"I really need your help. You're the senior military person in our state. As you may know, I ran on the flag issue."

Larry didn't know what the "flag issue" was, so he nodded and listened.

"I need to get the flag issue off the table," Barnes said.

"What are you talking about, sir?"

The "flag issue" was easily explained—Barnes was elected on his promise to remove the Confederate flag from the state flag of Georgia—but not as easily solved.

"I've got this idea," Barnes said.

"Okay ..."

"I'd like to put together a four-person panel. And I'd like for you to be on it," the governor said. "I've already asked President Carter, and he's agreed."

Barnes wanted Larry and President Carter to lead a road show across Georgia to drum up support for the removal of the Confederate flag.

"Governor, we really don't get into politics," Larry said. "That's not what I do, and I'd feel a little uncomfortable."

"Think about it."

"Let me talk to the Pentagon."

The response from Washington, D.C., surprised Larry.

"You're a big guy down there now," he was told. "If you choose to do it, it's up to you."

He spoke to his staff. And he called me.

"Felker, I don't know crap about this," he said.

"I think it'll be okay," I told him. "You can do some good for Georgia. You just have to consider your words and actions carefully."

Larry's discomfort with being out front on the flag issue was nonetheless high. He felt squeezed and thought long and hard about how to satisfy his competing constituencies.

"Governor," he said in a follow-up call, "I do not want to, and I will not get into state politics. But I'll be happy to speak about the military around the state of Georgia and anyplace else."

Barnes understood Larry's conflict.

"That will be fine," he said. "I just need your presence there."

Larry stood with President Carter at the Carter Center in Atlanta and a few other places. The press followed them to every stop. And while Larry never directly spoke out against the Confederate flag, his presence at the events conveyed a strong message.

29. OUR CHILDREN

I am blessed to be the father of four children: Michael, Wende, Jay and Wesley.

We are a truly modern family, too.

Michael was born in the same year that Mary and I married. Michael was my son. His mother, Rosa, and I dated when I was stationed in Texas, before I met Mary. Mary officially became Michael's stepmother, but we've always embraced him as our own child.

Early in our marriage, it became pretty clear that we could not have any children of our own. But we wanted children, so we set about qualifying ourselves for adoption. And we did. Felecia Wynette—whom we call "Wende"—joined us at just 14 days old; Felker William III—he goes by "Jay"—became a member of the family at 13 days; and Franklin Wesley, who is half-Korean and half African-American, came to us at age 3 while we were stationed in South Korea.

Our children fill what would have otherwise been a big void in our lives. They have been a wonderful blessing to us.

Notice, if you look at it, Felecia, Felker III and Franklin all have the same initials: FWW. That was my wife's genius idea in naming them.

Mary and I love and value each of our children equally and are so very proud of the men and woman they have become.

That said, our approach to child-rearing could often be at odds, as Mary will tell you.

"Felker could go and sit with these kids and they would just talk to him," she said. "Whatever I wanted to know, he said I could probably find out, if *I* would just listen long enough! I did too much talking. And

*Back row, from left: Mary Ward, Georgia Gov. George Busbee,
Felker Ward Jr.; front: Wende, Wesley, Jay.*

Felker did all of the listening. He was always close to the kids.

"He's just like his dad: supportive of all the children. And he is a forgiving person. He'll give a child enough rope to hang themselves. If he listens to you, then you've pretty much got him in your corner. He was very patient. Felker was fair. I think that I jumped to conclusions too fast."

I struggled with how to tell their stories as individual and unique members of the Ward Family until I found a solution: I invited them to be authors of their own tale, with only minor narratives from me.

MICHAEL WARD

Our eldest son, Michael, is a lawyer here in Atlanta.

Michael and his ex-wife have three children. Evan Michael graduated from the University of Michigan in 2016 with a degree in computer engineering. He's working in California for a tech company. Morgan is a student at Georgia State. And Michaela is in high school.

This is Michael's story, in his own words:

"I didn't grow up with my dad," he said. "I grew up with my mom, a stepdad and five older siblings. I grew up as the baby on my mom's side, and the oldest on my dad's side.

"As a 16-year-old, I met my dad and Mary for the first time—I call her my mom now, because she pretty much is my mom—and my younger siblings in Atlanta. My mom arranged it. We've been family ever since. I had the privilege of being a baby brother and a big brother.

"My mother, Rosa Stewart, was a beautiful woman who came from a big family herself. She was 'Miss Anderson High School' one year. She dated and wound up marrying the captain of the football team, a guy named William Hygh. They started having children and moved from Texas to California, where he accidentally drowned. By then she and William had five children. She was all of 28 years old. Still young, still pretty. She moved back to Austin, Texas, where she was from.

"She met my dad when he was there in Army flight school at San Marcos, which is a suburb outside of Austin. They met, they dated. She wound up having me on May 1, 1968, a week after her own birthday. She was not married then, mind you. I was child number six for her.

"Of course, my aunts and uncles, the older folks on my mom's side in Texas, all knew who my dad was. They'd all met him; they liked him. Eventually one of my few remaining maternal aunts showed me pictures of my mom and dad together. They all said good things about him. My oldest brother and oldest sister knew who he was. They were teenagers when he and my mom were dating in Texas. And they all respect him a great deal to this day. As do I.

"I remembered my dad's voice. I was just curious what he sounded like, what he looked like. Does he look like me? Do I look like him? I was asking all kinds of questions a young child would ask his mom about his dad around that time. My mom humored me. 'He looks just like you.' I said, 'He must be one handsome guy.' Which made her start laughing.

"We moved back in Pittsfield where I finished high school and at-

Michael Ward, Felker Ward Jr., Evan Michael Ward.

tended my first year of college at UMass, then went back to Texas.

"While I was in high school, my curiosity piqued. I said, 'Mom, I'd like to go meet my dad.'

"She picked up the phone, made a call. The next thing I knew, she arranged for me to go to Atlanta. I was 16, in the 11th grade. It was summertime when I met my dad for the first time. It was a new family for them and me. Their kids and I hit it off, right off the bat. They got a big brother now. And I got a little sister and two little brothers that I never had. We were all best buddies from day one. My dad and I had a spiritual and certainly genetic connection.

"The first thing my stepmom—Mary—said to me was, 'Yeah, you're Felker's child. Look at your knees!' I was the talk of the town at that point. She was on the phone with her family in Columbus. My sister and brothers were telling their friends in the neighborhood, 'We just met our big brother!' And Mom (Mary) was saying, 'I just met Felker's son. He looks just like him! He walks like him. His head's like him!'

"For the first time, I got a good sense of who my dad was, and what his character was about. In a small way, I saw myself when I looked at him. I saw a part of the future of my character in him. And he no doubt saw a lot of himself in me, I think, for the first time.

"We spent that summer, and pretty much every summer after that together. We grew as a family. I was the first of their kids that was old enough to drive his car. I started to see what the life of a lawyer was on those visits.

"Between my sophomore and junior years of college at the University of Texas, I decided I wanted to go to Atlanta and spend more time with my dad now. I applied to and was accepted at the University of Georgia. My dad helped me out with tuition.

"My mom was a bit skeptical about sending me to Atlanta. But I think there was vindication for my mom when I got back to Pittsfield from my first visit and she and my dad had a talk. She told me later, 'I talked to your dad and he thanked me for sending you down there. He said y'all had a good time and he wants to see you again. He also told me, "You've done a good job raising this child." ' She just beamed and smiled at hearing that from my dad after all those years. That was all she had to hear from him.

"My dad is a great guy. He's a Taurus, I'm a Taurus, my mom is a Taurus. I have a son that's a Taurus. We have a family full of Tauruses. A lot of us act and think and view the world alike. My mom and dad and I were no exception. All independent, a little headstrong sometimes. Persistent. We believe in taking care of home first. Work, make money, have a lot of love to give. Be loyal; be honest. And my dad's all that."

FELECIA "WENDE" WYNETTE WARD-LITTLE

Wende's a bright, loving person and we were fortunate to have her as the first baby growing up in our household. She set a high mark.

She was a beautiful child. You know how women have a habit of seeing a newborn baby and saying, "Isn't she cute?" Well, most of them aren't cute.

But this child was really cute. She was a beautiful child.

As eager as we were to have her, though, I have to admit we were not entirely prepared.

We were so excited when the adoption agency said we could take Wende, but we neglected to go to the store and buy diapers! We hadn't bought anything for the child, because we didn't think we were going to get her quite that fast. We went straight to Rich's, which was the big department store here at that time. It was my job to stay in the car and tend to our new daughter while Mary went shopping. I sat with her, alone in the parking lot, scared to *death* that this child was going to wake up! I would not have had any idea what to do if she started crying and screaming, as kids usually do. But my Wende? She was the perfect child for a new dad. She didn't wake up while we waited for Mary, and

Mary's father, John Jamerson, entertaining grandchildren Wende, left, and Jay.

everything turned out just fine.

We had built a modest three-bedroom home for us right next door to my parents' home in Northwest Atlanta. Together, my folks and Mary and I had bought some acreage. My mother and dad built a home on part of it and we built on another part.

Without telling them what we were up to, we got word to my parents to come over to our house.

"We've got something to show you!"

In walked my mother, and there's a baby in the living room! She was so surprised and so happy. Of course, she fell in love with Wende right off the bat.

Her first night under our roof, we had Wendy's crib set up in the bedroom right next to ours. She woke up that night—she either cried or whimpered—and Mary and I jumped out of bed in the dark and ran into each other at the door trying to be the first to see about this child. We had a big laugh about that.

From that moment forward, we agreed that we would decide ahead of time whose turn it was going to be to get up with Wende the next time she woke up during the night.

It was an exciting time for us.

"Once we got Wendy," Mary recalled, "Grandmama Ward became

176

our babysitter. I paid her to stay at home and keep the baby. She really enjoyed it. We always teased her because she would say, 'Don't spank Wende!' She had a nice soft voice as a granny. One day, Wende was tearing up Grandmama's flowers. I laughed and said, 'Don't spank Wende!' But Felker's mother was so perfect with that child. She would take her out every day regardless of the weather. Wende never got sick, never got colds or anything like that."

Wende attended Spelman College here in Atlanta. She was a real joy to us as she grew up and she is the mother to two of our five grandchildren, Maurissa and Kerrington.

This is Wende's story about growing up a Ward:

"My mother is a bridge player," she said. "When we were growing up, she played party bridge on Saturdays. My dad, meanwhile, hunted on Saturdays when we were kids, and he would have to babysit us some of those Saturdays. That meant that me and my two brothers had to go hunting! It also meant getting up early in the morning, packing a lunch and staying in the woods with him all day. I didn't really like it that much because I was a girl. But I went.

"I learned how to swim in Korea. I was just mortified to put my head under the water. I remember my dad kneeling down along the side of the pool in his uniform and telling me, 'You've got to do this. You've got to put your head in the water. It's part of swimming.' After 20 minutes of coaxing, I did it. I was good for the next swim class the next day. That's my earliest memory of my father.

"When we lived in Korea, I went pheasant hunting with him from time to time, which was a little different. We didn't have to walk the woods so much. I remember them taking us in a car and driving through wherever it was we were hunting and hopping out of the car to hunt.

"I didn't really like fishing a whole lot, either, at least when we were fishing on a lake. Because to me, fishing on a lake is slow, and you had to stay there all day in order to catch anything. What I did like was the deep-sea fishing that I experienced as a kid. We would fish on a boat in the Panhandle, in Destin, Florida, which meant getting up early in the morning. The farther out we went deep-sea fishing, the more seasick we kids became, but if we stayed along the shore and trolled for king mackerel, we could see the condos and the beaches and the people on the beaches. That was a lot of fun.

"Destin is in the Central time zone—an hour behind Atlanta. On one trip, my dad forgot to set the clocks to Florida time, so we got up an hour early. We gave him such a hard time about it; it was bad!

"My brothers and I had a lot of childhood experiences that the kids in our neighborhood didn't have. We felt very fortunate.

"My dad and my mother believed in spanking. My dad had us out one Sunday afternoon after church working in the garden. We all had something else—anything else—we wanted to do. But he had us hoeing up weeds around the beans and corn. He showed us what he wanted us to do. And for some stupid reason, we started hoeing up the vegetables. So he spanked all three of us. 'You guys know the difference between these vegetables and the weeds! I need you not to be hoeing up my vegetables!' We went right back to doing it again and hoed up *more* vegetables. And he spanked us *again*. We got a series of three spankings that day. I guess by the third time we learned our lesson.

"Now, of course, they don't believe in spanking their *grand*kids … My dad told me, 'You know, I'm not really sure that spanking did you guys any good, so I don't think you should spank your children.' And I looked at him like, 'Are you the same person that raised us? Are you serious?'

"My dad was not a mean person as a parent. Being a military man, he believed in order. He really tried to impress upon us that if you're early, you're on time. If you're on time, you're late. Being punctual was important in the Ward Family.

"My parents believed in discipline. We were accustomed to being punished or having privileges taken away. They did not reward bad behavior. My dad said that there's no reason to not make an 'A' in behavior. 'You can sit down and keep your mouth shut and get your work done,' he said. I was a talker in school. I remember my dad coming to my third-grade class one time in his uniform, unannounced. I was running my mouth and the other kids were doing their work. I was not doing mine. He looked at me like, 'What are you doing? Are you doing your work?' That weekend was the first slumber party I would have ever gone to. And because he saw, first-hand, that I wasn't doing my work, my punishment was that I didn't get to go.

"We were raised as if my mother gave birth to us. My father is the oldest of the three children that his parents had—three boys. When I came along, I was the first baby girl that my grandmother had her hands on. I never met a mother who had all girls that didn't want a son, or a mother that had all boys that didn't want a girl. I always knew that to my parents and to my paternal grandparents, I was special. We lived next door to them. They raised us in a way that we didn't see the difference between the three of us in terms of not actually being biologically theirs. We fiercely consider ourselves brothers and sister, because we were raised together.

"My father is a pastor's kid. The church that he grew up in was the Triumph Holiness Church and the Kingdom of God. They believed that

God spoke directly to them. I heard a lady minister talk to my dad one time and tell him that he was called to be a minister. But I don't think that my dad wanted to be confined to the four walls of the church and to a pulpit. When I think about all the places that he's been and all the things that he's done, he has effectively touched more people in his daily life throughout his lifetime than he ever could have touched from a pulpit. He has a great faith. He believes in prayer. We were raised to say our blessings at dinner, but also to say prayers at night before we went to bed. And my parents still kneel down next to their bed and say prayers at night before they go to sleep every night. They are Episcopalian now, so their religious experience has transitioned. But my dad believes in the power of prayer and they instilled that in us. We went to church as a family.

"Our friends used to kind of joke that we were like the Cleavers in the TV show 'Leave it to Beaver.' They thought we were different. They could remember coming to our house at dinnertime and we'd all be sitting around the table eating together, because we ate as a family. The only time that we didn't eat as a family was if my dad had a meeting or was out of town. And that did not happen often when we were kids. He was pretty much at home, working in the city, and was with us at dinnertime. It wasn't just a once-a-week thing. We ate most of our meals together as a family. It was a time when we could talk about our day.

"My friends knew my dad was a colonel and a lawyer, and some of them kind of feared him, because they felt talking to him was like being interrogated by Perry Mason. Maybe they weren't afraid of him, but he definitely intimidated a few of them. They knew that my dad always meant business. There was never a time when I thought he was like anybody else's dad.

"We talk about gun control now as an issue that is prevalent. But we grew up in a house where we understood you didn't touch the guns unless you had Dad's permission. He had a gun case where he displayed his hunting rifles. There was a lock on it, and most of the time the key was in the lock. But we never touched it, because we knew better.

"My dad sometimes said that he and Mom were not exactly on the same page in terms of how we were raised. My dad believed, 'The kids are going to make a certain number of mistakes. We're going to allow them to make mistakes and learn from their mistakes.' My mother's attitude was more, 'We need to tell them *exactly* what to do.' It was a difference in their own upbringings. My mother came from a family where they were pretty much told, 'You're going to do this this way, and you're going to do this that way.' My dad was a little bit more about free will and not so much direction. Mom felt like more direction was the order of the day.

"My dad's college roommate and business partner, Herman J. Russell, said to me, 'If you go to Tuskegee, I'll pay your tuition.' I thought hard about going to Tuskegee. But while Tuskegee was great as a little kid, I didn't think I could do it for school. I grew up in the city, so I stayed in Atlanta and went to Spelman.

"When we were told about Michael coming to Atlanta for the first time, I don't remember us having a whole lot of advance warning. We just knew that we had a big brother and he was coming to visit. As three little kids, Jay, Wes and I were super-excited. The night that he arrived, Dad picked him up from the airport. He learned about us on his ride from the airport to our house. When he arrived, we were jumping up and down, so excited! Mother had put us to bed, but the idea was that if we were still awake when Mike got there, we'd get a chance to meet him. And he said that he was just as excited to meet us, because he grew up in a family where he was the youngest. He was getting to come and meet his brothers and his sister for the first time. He said he was pretty stoked about it. We've never looked at Mike as being our half-brother or stepbrother or anything of that nature. He's our brother.

"My brothers and I are extremely close. We don't get together now as much as we used to but football draws us together a lot on Sundays. That is a lot of fun to have all of the sofa coaches and the cheering and the loud noise and laughter and all of that."

•••

Mary and I have been especially close to Wende's eldest daughter, Maurissa. We've carried her with us all over the world, from Australia to Alaska. She was the child of a man who showed little interest in being a father and we have always been partial to her. Some of our other grandchildren have said that! But it's true. My attitude was, *I'm the man in her life.* We're not at all reluctant to confess that we filled a void in her life. Michael has three children. They've got a full-time mother and father. Maurissa doesn't.

"When I got a spanking one time from my mother," Maurissa remembered, "I told on my mom to my grandparents. I never got another spanking after that."

When Maurissa was in elementary school, she stayed with us during the week and at Wende's house on the weekends. We were there for ballet recitals, piano concerts, violin concerts, volleyball games, everything. She returned to live with us when she started college. Even though she moved out to live on her own recently, she still talks to us

Granddaughter Maurissa Ward getting acquainted with a koala in Australia.

almost daily. When Mary and I attend functions related to many of the boards that I served on, Maurissa is almost always there with us.

From the time she was 10 years old, if my long-time secretary, Mattie Williams, needed time off during summers or after school,

Maurissa would come to the office and answer the phone for me. As she got older—and asked for a raise—I increased her responsibilities to filing papers and helping me sort out paperwork for my taxes. When I operated a medical clinic, AeroClinic at the airport, she worked in the office there, and again when we operated a duty-free shop, she worked for my son Jay, her uncle.

Every spring, our children and grandchildren join Mary and I at our house to plant corn, squash, cucumbers, blueberries and muscadines for homemade wine. On one occasion, we put the wine in bottles in the kitchen and it exploded overnight. Quite a mess! Mary wasn't angry, but she gave Maurissa and me a look that said, "Y'all are going to be cleaning this up. I'm not."

Every time I want to fix something, Maurissa will tease me and say, "Don't you think you should call a professional?"

"I don't need a professional," I tell her. "I know what I'm doing."

I taught Maurissa how to drive a car and a farm tractor, how to drive a boat and how to fish in both freshwater and salt. She joined Mary and me when we stayed on a boat in Valdez, Alaska, with Dean and Jan Owen. Another boat would come and meet us every day and take us out fishing. We talked about school, fishing and our military experiences. And Maurissa caught a 121-pound halibut.

"That was literally the most fun I've ever had ever with my grandfather," she said.

I told her, "If I help you reel in it, then you have to say that I helped you."

"Then I'll just do it by myself, because I don't want to have to give you any credit for this!"

Maurissa tends to be a bit impatient so I sometimes feel like I've given her the same advice every day: "Patience is a virtue."

She will also ask a million and one questions.

"Hey Poppy, can I ask you a question?"

"What do you want to ask?"

And then she'll ask two or three questions, one after the other, after the other.

"I thought you had one question."

"Yeah, I know," she'll say. "It started off with one question. But you know, it just developed into two or three more."

I VOTED
FOR A VERY
SPECIAL DAD
(NOMINEE: FELKER W.
WARD, JR.)
ON
FATHERS
DAY!

VOTES
○ PRES. REAGAN
○ JIMMY CARTER
● FELKER WARD, JR.
○ NIXON
○ IOTA
COMAINY

THESE ARE THE
REASONS WHY ───▷

OLM LAND
CITY

WHAT MAKES A ~~GOOD~~ REALLY GOOD DAD!

Dads have to be sweet,
and have corns on their feet.
They have to have a good song,
I guess we are some.
Please stay your self,
and stay in good health.

I CONGRADJULATE YOU ON
YOUR PROJECT. I HOPE THAT THEIR
ARE MORE WHERE THAT ONE ~~COM~~ CAME
FROM. PLEASE CONTINUE YOUR ~~SONG~~
SUCCESS IN BEING A FATHER
AND A GOOD ~~CO. CO~~ LAWYER.
FOR ALL OF THE THINGS ~~YOUG~~ YOU'VE
DONE FOR US I WOULD HAVE TO

BUY ABOUT FIRTHTEEN OR ~~MORE~~
MAJOR ~~CITE~~ CITIES TO REPAY YOU, NOW
I AM FINISHED WITH MY SPEECH AND
ALL I AM TRYING TO SAY IS THAT I
                                  LOVE YOU.

From one
of your to
Best Sons,
Love and
Compassion,

Jay
S.H.

P.S. HAPPY FATHERS
DAY

To a Very _Special_ Dad
On _Father's Day!_

REASONS (JUST SOME!)

①. You are a man of a great
many talents.

②. You support your family with
a strong had hand.

③. You have accomplished the goals
and _challenges_ set foward to you.

④. You have made me proud to
have the name "Felker W. Ward, III.

⑤. AND MOST OF ALL;
You are the Best Dad
The World has ever known!

FELKER "JAY" WARD III

With Wende, we'd made our application for adoption and the agency put Mary and me through all the hoops, making sure we offered an appropriate home for a child. Once we were approved, we waited until a baby came along that they thought would be a good fit for us. They let us come and see the child—Wende—and we did. They said, "Take three days to think it through and make sure that she is what you want, that this is the right child." We did that.

And then when Jay came along, we went through the same exercise. And we said, "Why do we need to wait three days? We see the baby, we want the baby, why can't we take him home today?"

And they let us do it.

Jay joined our family at 13 days of age a year after Wende; same process, same agency.

"Jay was always independent," Mary recalled. "He thought he could do whatever he wanted to do. By then we lived in southwest Atlanta, probably a good 10 minutes south of Interstate 20. Felker's parents lived in northwest Atlanta. If Jay got upset with somebody because they didn't let him do what he wanted to do, he would think that he could just walk off and go home by himself! Another time, when we were in Korea, he tried his best to leave school and walk home. He was forever determined to have his way."

He had to wear glasses as a fairly young child. Children come into their own at different times, different ages. Some earlier than others. Jay matured more slowly physically and psychologically than Wende did. He had had all sorts of problems with his tonsils and often ran a fever. There were times we had to put him in cold water to bring his body temperature down to normal.

As children will do, he ultimately outgrew his early challenges and developed into a fine and healthy young man.

Jay attended Morehouse College before transferring to Mercer University, where he earned a bachelor's degree in business administration. He was always working, always ambitious, and eventually became a management trainee for our company, Concessions International.

That put him in good stead years later when he created a company of his own, Trans-Air Concessions, LLC. I'm now a minority shareholder in the company. He has been a very successful entrepreneur.

Jay worked for Concessions International for a number of years and learned the business from us. And now I'm working for him, in a sense. He has some businesses in airports, and I've backed him a little on the financial side and advice.

Jay said his earliest memories are of my Army service.

"I remember that Dad worked long, hard hours. He was gone quite often, but when he was home it was always family time. We took trips together as a family; he always focused his life around us.

"The friends that he had, the company that he kept, were always memorable. I just thought that they were regular folks, but to the world they turned out to be giants. When we were younger, we used to have an attorney come to our house quite often and stay with us sometimes through the weekend. We just knew he was from L.A. The attorney turned out to be Johnnie Cochran. As I got older, Maynard Jackson—the mayor of Atlanta!—came to our house quite a bit seeking my dad's counsel on different things. So did Georgia Gov. Joe Frank Harris. Andy Young would come over quite a bit, too."

Jay worked as a bartender during college and for years after. He learned the ropes by mixing drinks for my visiting friends.

When Jay and Wes were in high school, Mary and I had 15 head of cattle at one point. The boys—and to some extent Mike when he moved to Atlanta—spent a lot of time on the weekends tending to my farm with him, from running fence wire to preparing cattle for castration.

"We loved being around Dad," Jay said. "As teenagers, our friends would be off doing other things on the weekends, and we had conflicts sometimes. But we always supported our father and helped him. Even though sometimes, yeah, we would have a kind of snarl on our face. Or we'd say, 'At 5, Dad, I've got to go because I'm going to the movies.' We never said no to hard work; we were never disobedient. And we all reaped the rewards of that labor. The reason I like vegetables now is because we had fresh vegetables growing up."

I loved all my kids but I was not the kind of father who would spoil them. They had jobs; do your job, get your allowance, that was my rule.

When Jay was 15, he talked to me about getting a car when he turned 16. Most of the parents of his classmates were buying cars for them.

"I'll make you a deal," I told him. "Whatever you earn and save from working this summer, I'll double your money, and we'll get you a car that way."

Jay saved $2,800 and, as promised, Mary and I matched it.

"It showed me the value of working hard for something," Jay said. "I took care of it like it was a brand-new car. Some of the lessons like that he taught us along the way are invaluable today."

After college, Jay went to work for Concessions International in Los Angeles. He spent two years there and five more in Seattle. When we finally won an airport concessions contract at Atlanta-Hartsfield International Airport, he returned home to work at the corporate office.

There was, however, an incident in 1998 that caused some turbulence in my professional relationship with my son. Jay decided to share this story, so I'll let him tell it in his own words:

"When I was working in Seattle," he said, "there was a situation where some of the management team came to me secretly in a meeting and said, 'Why is it that the assistant managers in this company and line concourse managers are not bonused? Why is the GM is the only person at the branch that gets a bonus?'

"I said, 'I don't know; that's the way it's always been.'

"They knew that I could have one of the owner's ears—my dad's— on this particular subject. I did my research about different companies and their processes with bonuses. I came to the same conclusion that our managers had. And they weren't alone. There were others echoing the same sentiment. Our general manager got wind of it and said, 'It's not going to happen.'

"I elevated the situation and talked to my father about it. I said, 'I think it makes sense for us to look at this because we're going to lose talented guys who want to grow with the company, but who will leave because they'll be better compensated at another company.'

"My dad agreed. He did the research and came to the conclusion that we needed to spread the bonuses a little bit further than just to general managers. He took it to the other principals and the board, and he convinced them that it was the right thing to do. That was a win. I thought, 'I've done something good for the company.'

"My father came back to me and said, 'Listen. We've decided to give these bonuses, but I want you to keep a lid on it. Don't tell anybody until we announce it. It's important that you not tell anybody.'

"A month passed by and the general manager at my location felt a little threatened. He had gotten wind that the assistant managers had started a conversation about the bonus program. He showed me a bit of animosity. We were still getting along pretty well, but it was becoming contentious.

"In a meeting one day, I let him know that maybe everybody is going to get bonuses. Of course, my father told me not to say anything about the bonuses. It got back to him that the cat had been let out of the bag by me. Which was true.

"I apologized for it.

"He said, 'I told you not to do that.'

"I said, 'He made me mad. He said something rude to me. And that's when I said it.'

"Dad said, 'Well, I'm really disappointed by this. It's not the worst thing in the world. But I can't trust you. You've got to do better than that.'

"As a result, two years later, when my dad and Jesse Hill sold their shares of Concessions International to Herman J. Russell, I was caught completely unaware. The bonus issue was the reason my dad didn't warn me that the sale was coming.

"'I didn't know if you could keep it to yourself,' he said.

"That hurt, but I understood; I hurt him by revealing something he told me not to share. More than 15 years later, it still hurts me that I hurt him. I didn't like disappointing him. It never happened again."

That was a tough time for both of us. I appreciated that Jay owned up to and learned from his mistake, however. He's a good man and his intentions were never in doubt.

FRANKLIN WESLEY "WES" WARD

We adopted Wesley from the Pearl S. Buck Foundation in South Korea. He was 3 years old. Wende and Jay went through the whole process of adoption with us. We discussed it, and we made the visits together.

When we got back to the United States, there was a little boy next door the same age as Wes, and they're friends to this day.

Wesley is a golfer, an excellent athlete and, after a run at the pro tour, he's in sales.

He received a bachelor's in business administration from Mercer and also earned an MBA from Mercer.

Wende, Jay and Wes all went to Woodward Academy, an Atlanta-based college prep school. Wende went to Woodward because she was dyslexic, and Woodward had an excellent program for mainstreaming dyslexic children. Once we had her in Woodward, it didn't make sense for us to have our other two children going somewhere else. It was a financial challenge for us because I was still on active duty in the Army. But I have no regrets about it. We're glad we spent the money.

On the academic front, Wesley was good. And on the athletic front, he was real good. He was a pitcher and a home-run hitter for the base-ball team. He was a varsity quarterback for the football team. After school, he wanted to make a career playing golf and we sponsored him for two years as he pursued his dream. Mary and I made a deal with Wes: Play seven days a week and we will take care of your expenses for two years. He made a couple of tournament cuts, so we extended our agreement with him for six more months.

When Wes joined the family, incidentally, it hadn't really occurred to any of us that he didn't speak English! That was a little bit of a bump

A man and his sons, from left: Michael, me, Wesley, Jay.

that everybody had to work through.

Here is my youngest son's story, told in his own words:

"I didn't know the English language. My first days with the family were with a Korean housekeeper who helped me get adjusted. I communicated with her in Korean. What I was told later was that I would curse in Korean, and the nanny was the only one that understood it. And she would spank me!

"We were never really in the same school building until I got to ninth grade. And then Jay and Wende and I were all in the same building. Jay was a junior, Wende was a senior. At that point, they kind of looked after me, and doted on me a little bit as their younger brother.

"Wende says that I'm her favorite brother, and I tend to agree. I should be! She's always had an eye out for me. Even now, because I guess in her eyes, I am still the baby. And the youngest.

"My dad being from the military—and just his general upbringing—meant he played the role of disciplinarian. There were consequences to what we did.

"There were always high expectations for us. Education was important and was always preached. My mom was a teacher.

"I got in trouble in high school. We went to Woodward Academy, which is a prestigious private boarding school in the Southeast. Back then, there weren't many minorities that went to that school because one, you had to test your way in. And two, it was quite expensive.

Education was important enough to our parents that they wanted us to have the best possible. I played sports—baseball and football—so I was kind of popular in that respect. But in my junior year, I got in trouble with some other teammates on the baseball team to the point where four of us, including myself, were dismissed from the school. Every spring the baseball team would go on a spring training camp trip to Florida. We did some stuff that we weren't supposed to do.

"Our team stayed at a hotel next to the training facility for the Houston Astros. The Astros were there at the same time. A few of our baseball players decided one night to break into the Astros' facility and steal some equipment— gloves, shoes, maybe a hat. They brought it back, and I took some of it.

"Word eventually got out to the teachers, the dean and, ultimately, the president of the academy. The people who were involved that either broke in and took some of the equipment—or people like myself that received some of the stolen equipment—went in front of the honor council and explained what they did. It was a crime, breaking and entering. And we transported stolen property across state lines. Which, at that time, I had no clue about. The Houston Astros didn't prosecute, so it was all a school disciplinary action. The people that broke in and took the equipment didn't tell anybody. They tried to cover it up and hide it. But it got out when one of the baseball team's players told his mom, who was a teacher at the school. She told the dean and the president.

"I was in deep trouble. I was freaked out of my mind. I had to go home and tell them what happened. The school called my parents and let them know. 'What am I going to do? What are they going to do to me? What are they going to say?' I was downstairs in my bedroom, freaked out, upset. My dad came into my room. He gave me a hug. He was calm, understanding and compassionate. He said, 'Just because you made a bad decision doesn't make you a bad person.'

"That was a big learning moment for me. I wasn't expecting that. I've carried that moment throughout my life. That's one moment that stuck with me.

"A nervous week went by and the decision came back that we would be expelled from school. My dad stood up for me even though I made a mistake. He had a problem with the school because there were other incidents that were far worse than theft when the kids involved were not expelled. There were kids selling drugs at school, for example.

"My dad asked, 'How could Wes be expelled for something far less serious than that?'

"The administration agreed to let me have a private tutor to finish out the year, and the credits I earned from the private tutor would count toward my junior year. I stayed on track and returned in the fall to finish my senior year at Woodward. I even played quarterback for the football team. That was a result of my dad standing up for me.

"And when it was over and settled, it was done as far as my parents went: 'We've resolved this. Let's move on and put it behind us.'

"My dad introduced me to the game of golf on vacation in Florida. Every summer, he played and he would take Jay and me with him on the course. He showed me how to hold a club and what clubs to hit with for what distance. But I never took up the game until my best friend, Roland Blanding, started playing. He knew more about the sport than I did. I knew that I was a better athlete than he was, but he always beat me at golf, which I didn't like! I started practicing on my own, so I could beat him. Eventually, it got to the point where I could beat him on a regular basis. That's what hooked me.

"My dad actually agreed to back me as I attempted to make it on the pro tour in my early 20s. He was my sponsor. He and Mom have always been supportive of anything that we wanted to do, academically or athletically.

"Golf became my job; that was my profession for several years.

"I get mistaken for Tiger Woods all the time. I've had people follow me around grocery stores and stop me on the highway and slam their brakes. 'Oh, my God, Tiger!' No, I'm not Tiger.

"One of the things that always fascinated me about my dad is him being as successful as he is without taking accounting courses growing up or having any financial background. He was always able to figure things out intuitively. To me, he was a genius. He didn't have algebra or calculus in school, but he figured out questions when we would ask him about our homework. 'How did you get to the answer?' I'd wonder. He could always figure problems out without really knowing how to do it.

"I was excited to find out we had an older brother but even more excited when he would come into town to visit. I was always excited to see him, excited to know he was coming. And glad when he was here. You could call him a gift.

"Mike and I are probably the most similar in personality, even though we never grew up together. We've got the same sense of humor. We're both business-minded. We both like sports more so than Jay does.

"Mike and I are huge college football fans as well. The entire family rallies around football games and football Sundays. Mike and I jab each other during college football season because of our respective University of Miami and University of Texas affiliations.

"Family is important to our parents, and they've made sure that we've always understood that. When kids get to adulthood, they kind of wander around and go their separate ways. Some eventually come back; some don't. But no matter where we are physically or emotionally, Mom and Dad want us to make an effort to spend time together. Because you only have one mother; you only have one father. You should always be able to depend on your family, because you can't depend on your friends the same way. We're fortunate that we all live in the same city. As we all get older, we value time together much more now.

"When I was 16, two weeks after I got my driver's license, I was in a car accident. The car was totaled. I called my dad's office to let him know. I talked to his assistant, Mattie Williams. I didn't tell Mattie I was in an accident. I just asked to speak to him. She said, 'He's in a meeting.' I said, 'Okay. Tell him I was in a car accident, and he can call me back.' He was so upset about that! That I was in an accident, of course, but he was more upset that I didn't interrupt his meeting to let him know! His point was, 'No matter how busy I am, or how important you think what I'm doing is, if one of the children calls, please interrupt and get me on the phone!' "

APPENDIX A: ADDITIONAL PHOTOGRAPHS

In this section, I have included a number of additional photographs from my family life and career.

A Ward and Jamerson family reunion.

Felker Ward Jr. with his wife, Mary, and Georgia Gov. George Busbee.

Felker prepares to take off in his Cessna 421.

APPENDIX B: AWARDS, CITATIONS, RECOGNITION

In this section, I have included images of a number of military awards and civilian honors that I have received during my career.

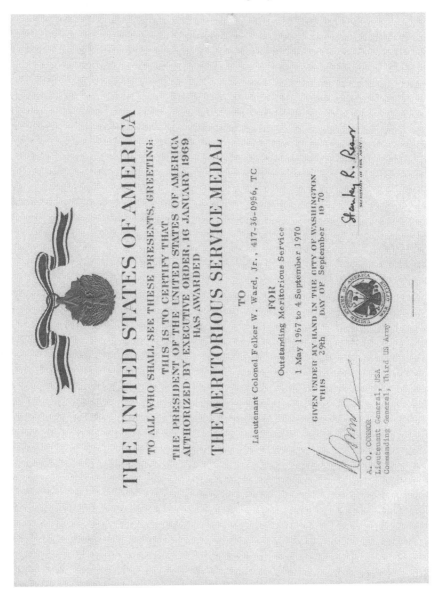

THE UNITED STATES OF AMERICA

TO ALL WHO SHALL SEE THESE PRESENTS, GREETING:

THIS IS TO CERTIFY THAT

THE PRESIDENT OF THE UNITED STATES OF AMERICA
AUTHORIZED BY EXECUTIVE ORDER, 16 JANUARY 1969
HAS AWARDED

THE MERITORIOUS SERVICE MEDAL

(FIRST OAK LEAF CLUSTER)

TO

LIEUTENANT COLONEL FELKER W. WARD, JR., 417-36-0956, TC

FOR

Outstanding Meritorious Service

3 April 1971 to 31 October 1972

GIVEN UNDER MY HAND IN THE CITY OF WASHINGTON

THIS   31st   DAY OF   October   19   72

Robert F. Froehlke

SECRETARY OF THE ARMY

MELVIN ZAIS

Lieutenant General, USA
Commander, Third U.S. Army

C I T A T I O N

BY DIRECTION OF THE PRESIDENT
THE AIR MEDAL
(SECOND OAK LEAF CLUSTER)
IS PRESENTED TO

MAJOR FELKER W. WARD, 097647, INFANTRY

UNITED STATES ARMY

For distinguishing himself by meritorious achievement while participating in sustained aerial flight in support of combat ground forces of the Republic of Vietnam during the period 21 May 1966 to 31 May 1966.

During this time he actively participated in more than twenty-five aerial missions over hostile territory in support of counterinsurgency operations. During all of these missions he displayed the highest order of air discipline and acted in accordance with the best traditions of the service. By his determination to accomplish his mission in spite of the hazards inherent in repeated aerial flights over hostile territory and by his outstanding degree of professionalism and devotion to duty, he has brought credit upon himself, his organization, and the military service.

The President of the United States of America, authorized by Executive Order, 16 January 1969, has awarded the Meritorious Service Medal (First Oak Leaf Cluster) to

LIEUTENANT COLONEL FELKER W. WARD, JR., 417-36-0956, TC

for outstanding meritorious service while assigned as Assistant Information Officer, Headquarters, Third United States Army, Fort McPherson, Georgia, from 3 April 1971 to 31 October 1972. During this period, Colonel Ward's performance of duty was marked by his outstanding dedication, integrity, and ability to establish and maintain a close rapport with all elements of the civilian and military communities. Through his ability to present the Army story clearly, forcefully and in a manner designed to engender public support of military programs, he was able to prepare for general officers of the headquarters an imposing number of speeches which were delivered in the public domain and which elicited much favorable response. As the delegated representative of the Third US Army Information Officer in all matters pertaining to the Fort McPherson Information Program, he rendered outstanding service to the installation and its commander through his diligent efforts in behalf of the establishment of an Atlanta Area-Fort McPherson Advisory Council and a Post Race Relations Council. Colonel Ward's outstanding performance of duty throughout this period represents achievement in the most cherished traditions of the United States Army and reflects the utmost credit upon himself and the Third United States Army.

Citation

BY DIRECTION OF THE PRESIDENT
THE AIR MEDAL
(SECOND OAK LEAF CLUSTER)
IS PRESENTED TO

MAJOR FELKER W. WARD 097647 INFANTRY
UNITED STATES ARMY

For distinguishing himself by meritorious achievement while participating in sustained aerial flight in support of combat ground forces of the Republic of Vietnam during the period 21 May 1966 to 31 May 196.

During this time he actively participated in more than twenty-five aerial missions over hostile territory in support of counterinsurgency operations. During all of these missions he displayed the highest order of air discipline and acted in accordance with the best traditions of the service. By his determination to accomplish his mission in spite of the hazards inherent in repeated aerial flights over hostile territory and by his outstanding degree of professionalism and devotion to duty, he has brought credit upon himself, his organization, and the military service.

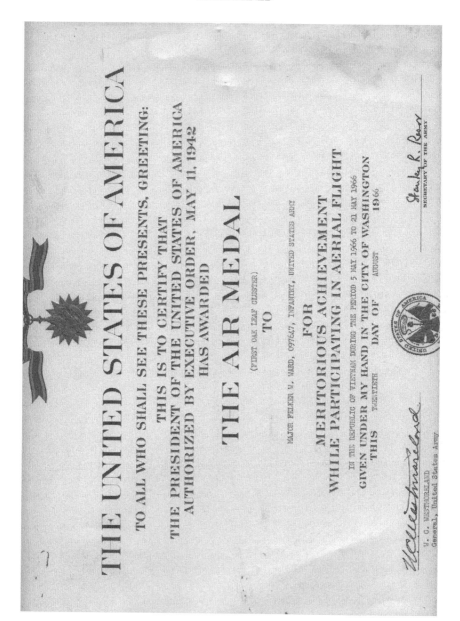

THE UNITED STATES OF AMERICA

TO ALL WHO SHALL SEE THESE PRESENTS, GREETING:

THIS IS TO CERTIFY THAT

THE PRESIDENT OF THE UNITED STATES OF AMERICA
AUTHORIZED BY EXECUTIVE ORDER, MAY 11, 1942

HAS AWARDED

THE AIR MEDAL

(FIRST OAK LEAF CLUSTER)

TO

MAJOR FELKER W. WARD, 097647, INFANTRY, UNITED STATES ARMY

FOR

MERITORIOUS ACHIEVEMENT
WHILE PARTICIPATING IN AERIAL FLIGHT

IN THE REPUBLIC OF VIETNAM DURING THE PERIOD 5 MAY 1966 TO 21 MAY 1966

GIVEN UNDER MY HAND IN THE CITY OF WASHINGTON

THIS   TWENTIETH   DAY OF   AUGUST   1966

W. C. Westmoreland
W. C. WESTMORELAND
General, United States Army

Stanley R. Resor
SECRETARY OF THE ARMY

CERTIFICATE OF APPRECIATION

FOR SERVICE IN THE ARMED FORCES OF THE UNITED STATES

LIEUTENANT COLONEL FELKER W. WARD JR, US ARMY, FROM 30 SEPTEMBER 1953 THRU 31 MARCH 1974

I extend to you my personal thanks and the sincere appreciation of a grateful nation for your contribution of honorable service to our country. You have helped maintain the security of the nation during a critical time in its history with a devotion to duty and a spirit of sacrifice in keeping with the proud tradition of the military service.

I trust that in the coming years you will maintain an active interest in the Armed Forces and the purpose for which you served.

My best wishes to you for happiness and success in the future.

Richard Nixon

COMMANDER IN CHIEF

BOARD OF OFFENDER REHABILITATION

A RESOLUTION

WHEREAS, the Honorable Felker W. Ward, Jr. was appointed as a member of the State Board of Offender Rehabilitation on April 10, 1980; and

WHEREAS, this outstanding Georgian served on the State Board of Offender Rehabilitation, and as Chairperson of its Fiscal Operations and Administration Committee, until November 5, 1981; and

WHEREAS, he provided expertise, understanding, and compassion in matters affecting the operations and administration of the Georgia Department of Offender Rehabilitation; and

WHEREAS, his deeds and accomplishments have been recorded in the annals of the minutes of the State Board of Offender Rehabilitation.

NOW THEREFORE, BE IT RESOLVED that the members of the State Board of Offender Rehabilitation hereby express their deep appreciation for the contributions of Mr. Felker W. Ward, Jr. to the Georgia correctional system, and wish for him continued success and happiness in the future.

BE IT FURTHER RESOLVED that a copy of this Resolution be furnished to the Honorable Felker W. Ward, Jr., and that a copy of this Resolution be made a part of the official minutes of the State Board of Offender Rehabilitation.

THIS _5th_ DAY OF _January_ , 1982.

Reverend E. C. Tillman, Chairperson

Mr. Joe C. Underwood

Mr. Norman Cavender

Mr. Bill Hutson

Mr. Preston N. Rawlins, Jr.

Mrs. Selina B. Stanford

Mrs. Cynthia W. Strong, Secretary

Mr. Edwin S. Varner, Jr., Vice-Chairperson

206

Tuskegee University

By authority of the Board of Trustees and upon recommendation
of the faculty, Tuskegee University hereby confers upon

Felker W. Ward, Jr.

the Degree

Doctor of Laws

Honoris Causa

with all the rights, honors, and privileges appertaining thereto.

Given at Tuskegee, Alabama, the sixth day of November, Two Thousand and Five.

_____
Chairman, Board of Trustees

_____
President

_____
Registrar

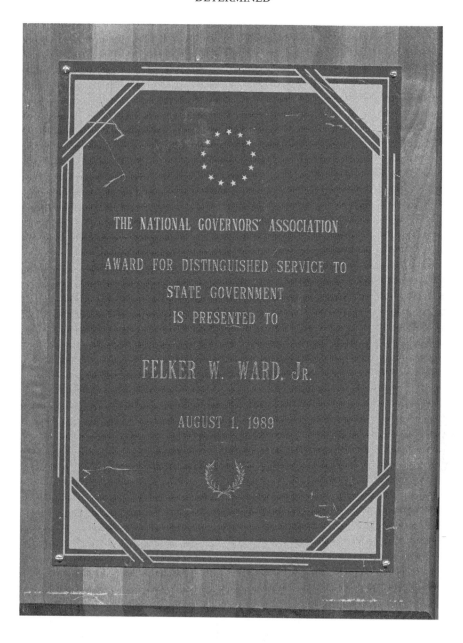

THE EMORY LAW ALUMNI ASSOCIATION

FELKER W. WARD, JR.

Commanding presence, trailblazer, trusted advisor and friend:

Whether the setting is flight school, law practice, or the business world, you pilot the enterprise... at the pinnacle of the field.

We know you as a leader among leaders, a wise and reliable counselor, one whom other leaders — in government, law, education, or high finance — turn to for advice.

They, like us, entrust you with their cares and their consciences... their corporate governance, their financial futures, their civic and personal trust.

We applaud you for your service and your accomplishments... your quiet reason, personal integrity, dignity, and forbearance... in short, for the content of your character.

We are glad you are among us. We are honored to present to you this Distinguished Alumnus Award.

_____
Dean, Emory School of Law

_____
President, Emory Law Alumni Association

About the Author

Felker W. Ward Jr. is a principal in the investment advisory firm of Pinnacle Investment Advisors, LLC, located in Atlanta, Georgia.

He retired from the Army in 1974 in the grade of Lieutenant Colonel (20 years' service). Most of his military career was spent as a pilot, logistics officer and public affairs officer. He started his legal career immediately upon retirement. For 10 years, he was a partner in the law firm of Kutak Rock & Campbell in Atlanta, engaged primarily in business and corporate law. He also served as Managing Partner of Kutak's Atlanta office.

Mr. Ward formed Ward and Associates, Inc. (later renamed Ward Bradford & Co., L.P.) in 1988, and Pinnacle Investment Advisors in 1991.

He received many awards and recognition for his accomplishments both during his military and business careers. Included in his military awards are the Vietnam Cross of Gallantry and the Legion of Merit.

About the Co-Author

Bob Andelman is the author or co-author of 16 books, ranging in topics from biography and business to crime and sports. Titles include: *Built From Scratch*, written with the co-founders of The Home Depot, Bernie Marcus and Arthur Blank; *Building Atlanta*, with Herman J. Russell; *Fans Not Customers* with Vernon Hill; *Mean Business* with "Chainsaw" Albert J. Dunlap; *The Profit Zone* with Adrian J. Slywotzky; *The Wawa Way* with Howard Stoeckel; *The Profiler* with Pat Brown; *Mind Over Business* with Ken Baum; *Bankers Not Brokers* with Merlin Gackle; *The Corporate Athlete* with Jack Groppel; *Keep Your Eye on the Marshmallow* with Joachim de Posada; and *The Consulate* (fiction) with Thomas R. Stutler. He is the sole author of: *Will Eisner: A Spirited Life*; *Why Men Watch Football*; and *Stadium For Rent*.

He is also the host and producer, since 2007, of the video podcast Mr. Media® Interviews (https://mrmedia.com)

For more information, please visit https://andelman.com

Twitter: @andelman

Facebook: https://facebook.com/andelman

Index

Made in the USA
Columbia, SC
25 August 2019